Six Sigma Black Belt Exam Prep

350 Practice Questions

Exam Code: CLSSBB-001

1st Edition

www.versatileread.com

Copyright © 2024 VERSAtile Reads. All rights reserved.
This material is protected by copyright, any infringement will be dealt with legal and punitive action.

Document Control

Proposal Name	:	Six Sigma Black Belt Exam Prep: 350 Practice Questions
Document Edition	:	1st
Document Release Date	:	14th November 2024
Reference	:	CLSSBB-001
VR Product Code	:	202447026SigmaBB

Copyright © 2024 VERSAtile Reads.

Registered in England and Wales

www.versatileread.com

All rights reserved. No part of this book may be reproduced or transmitted in any form or by any means, electronic or mechanical, including photocopying, recording, or by any information storage and retrieval system, without the written permission from VERSAtile Reads, except for the inclusion of brief quotations in a review.

Scan Me

Feedback:

If you have any comments regarding the quality of this book or otherwise alter it to better suit your needs, you can contact us through email at info@versatileread.com

Please make sure to include the book's title and ISBN in your message.

Copyright © 2024 VERSAtile Reads. All rights reserved.

This material is protected by copyright, any infringement will be dealt with legal and punitive action.

Voice of the Customer: Thank you for choosing this VersatileRead.com product! We highly value your feedback and insights via email to info@versatileread.com. As a token of appreciation, an amazing discount for your next purchase will be sent in response to your email.

Copyright © 2024 VERSAtile Reads. All rights reserved.
This material is protected by copyright, any infringement will be dealt with legal and punitive action.

About the Contributor:

Muniza Kamran

Muniza Kamran is a technical content developer in a professional field. She crafts clear and informative content that simplifies complex technical concepts for diverse audiences, with a passion for technology. Her expertise lies in Quality Management, Microsoft, cybersecurity, cloud security and emerging technologies, making her a valuable asset in the tech industry. Her dedication to quality and accuracy ensures that her writing empowers readers with valuable insights and knowledge. She has done certification in SQL database, database design, cloud solution architecture, and NDG Linux unhatched from CISCO.

Table of Contents

About Six Sigma Black Belt Certification 7
   Introduction 7
   What is a Six Sigma Black Belt? 7
   Certified Six Sigma Black Belt 8
      Requirements 8
      Preparation 8
      Certification 8
   Why Become a Certified Six Sigma Black Belt? 9
   Benefits of Black Belt Certification 9
   Career Opportunities for a Certified Six Sigma Black Belt 9
   What is the Salary of a Six Sigma Black Belt? 10
Practice Questions 11
Answers 92
About Our Products 161

About Six Sigma Black Belt Certification

Introduction

The Lean Six Sigma Black Belt (LSSBB) Handbook is designed for individuals who have already gained experience as Six Sigma Green Belts or equivalent, focusing on advanced tools and methodologies required for LSSBB certification. It builds on core content from previous belts, introducing new nonstatistical tools like 5S and Value Stream Mapping, and statistical tools like ANOVA and Regression Analysis. The book is organized to provide a comprehensive framework for Lean and Six Sigma, beginning with an overview and history, followed by Lean theories, and culminating in advanced problem-solving techniques. Aimed at preparing LSSBBs to manage complex projects and guide lower belt levels, the handbook is structured to be accessible across organizational hierarchies and industries, with step-by-step roadmaps like DMADV to support effective problem-solving. Six Sigma Black Belt Exam Cram by VERSAtile Reads serves as your comprehensive guide to achieving Six Sigma Black Belt certification. This certification elevates your expertise in process improvement, enabling you to lead strategic initiatives and drive meaningful change within your organization. Before diving into the specifics of Black Belt certification, let's explore the foundational principles of Six Sigma that will underpin your journey toward mastery.

What is a Six Sigma Black Belt?

A Six Sigma Black Belt is a professional with advanced expertise in Six Sigma methodologies and the ability to lead and mentor teams in implementing process improvement projects. Black Belts are critical to an organization's success, as they possess a deep understanding of both the theoretical and practical aspects of Six Sigma. They serve as change agents, guiding organizations in their pursuit of quality excellence.

Black Belts are responsible for managing complex projects, utilizing advanced statistical tools, and mentoring Green Belts and other team members. They work collaboratively with cross-functional teams to drive continuous improvement initiatives, ensuring that projects align with organizational goals and objectives.

Certified Six Sigma Black Belt

The IASSC Certified Six Sigma Black Belt™ (ICBB™) designation signifies a professional's mastery of Six Sigma principles and methodologies. Black Belts lead process improvement projects, demonstrating a comprehensive understanding of the DMAIC phases as outlined in the IASSC Six Sigma Black Belt Body of Knowledge™.

The IASSC Certified Six Sigma Black Belt Exam consists of 150 multiple-choice questions with a duration of 4 hours. The exam is closed-book and proctored, assessing candidates' knowledge of Six Sigma concepts, tools, and techniques. Achieving a passing score of 70% is required to earn certification.

Requirements

Candidates seeking IASSC Black Belt certification do not need any prerequisites, making it accessible to professionals at various stages in their careers. However, prior experience in Lean Six Sigma projects and an understanding of basic statistical concepts are highly beneficial.

Preparation

While formal training is not mandatory, it is highly recommended for candidates to engage in comprehensive training programs to prepare effectively for the exam. Many candidates find value in practicing with sample questions and assessments to gauge their readiness. The IASSC offers an informal (non-proctored) Black Belt Evaluation Exam to help candidates assess their knowledge and skills.

Certification

Upon passing the exam, candidates receive an IASSC Black Belt Certification, validating their proficiency in Six Sigma methodologies. This certification remains valid indefinitely, with a "Current" status for three years. To maintain this status, professionals are encouraged to engage in continuous learning and apply Six Sigma principles in their work.

Certified Black Belts receive a certificate (PDF), a badge (.png file), and recognition on the Official IASSC Certification Register, allowing them to showcase their expertise in Six Sigma on resumes and professional profiles.

Why Become a Certified Six Sigma Black Belt?

Pursuing a Six Sigma Black Belt certification is an excellent choice for professionals committed to leading process improvement initiatives and driving organizational change. Black Belts possess the skills to analyze complex data, implement advanced statistical techniques, and lead cross-functional teams in achieving process excellence.

Black Belt certification is ideal for experienced professionals in management, quality assurance, engineering, and operations who aspire to enhance their leadership capabilities and contribute to strategic initiatives within their organizations. This certification empowers candidates to take on roles that require a high level of expertise in process improvement and project management.

Benefits of Black Belt Certification

- **Enhanced Leadership Skills:** Develop advanced leadership and mentoring capabilities to drive successful improvement initiatives.
- **Increased Earning Potential:** Black Belts command higher salaries due to their specialized skills and contributions to organizational success.
- **Strategic Influence:** Position yourself as a key contributor to organizational strategy and decision-making processes.
- **Broader Career Opportunities:** Open doors to advanced roles in quality management, operations, and process improvement across various industries.

Career Opportunities for a Certified Six Sigma Black Belt

Six Sigma Black Belts can pursue various roles across industries, taking on responsibilities that involve leading complex projects, mentoring teams, and driving continuous improvement. Common job titles include:

- **Six Sigma Black Belt:** Responsible for leading and managing Six Sigma projects and initiatives.
- **Process Improvement Manager:** Oversees process improvement strategies and initiatives, ensuring alignment with organizational goals.
- **Quality Manager:** Develops and implements quality management systems and processes, ensuring compliance with industry standards.
- **Operational Excellence Manager:** Drives operational excellence initiatives across departments, fostering a culture of continuous improvement.
- **Project Manager:** Manages complex projects using Six Sigma methodologies to achieve defined goals and objectives.
- **Lean Six Sigma Consultant:** Provides expert guidance on Lean Six Sigma principles to organizations seeking process improvement.
- **Data Analyst:** Analyzes data to identify trends and opportunities for improvement using statistical tools and techniques.
- **Business Process Analyst:** Evaluates and optimizes business processes, ensuring efficiency and quality.

What is the Salary of a Six Sigma Black Belt?

Certified Six Sigma Black Belts are in high demand, and their expertise often leads to lucrative career opportunities. The average salary for a Six Sigma Black Belt varies by industry and experience level. On average, Black Belts earn between $90,000 and $130,000 annually, with potential for higher earnings in management and specialized roles.

Practice Questions

1. What is the primary focus of Lean Six Sigma (LSS)?

   a. Management of business departments

   b. Management of organizational processes

   c. Individual performance metrics

   d. Short-term financial gains

2. Why is process ownership essential in LSS?

   a. To replace the traditional management hierarchy

   b. To ensure a cross-functional focus for process success

   c. To increase competition among departments

   d. To delegate responsibilities to lower-level managers

3. How is a process owner selected in LSS?

   a. Through a voting process by employees

   b. By the amount of resources they control

   c. By top management after identifying and defining the process

   d. Randomly from a pool of managers

4. What is the role of the Process Management Committee (PMC)?

   a. To perform day-to-day operations

   b. To manage individual departments

   c. To collectively share responsibilities related to process management

   d. To replace the process owner when necessary

Practice Questions

5. Who heads the Process Management Committee (PMC)?

a. The functional owner

b. The general manager

c. The focus owner

d. The CEO

6. What is a key characteristic of the members of the PMC?

a. They are from the same department

b. They are peer-level managers

c. They are lower-level managers

d. They are external consultants

7. Which of the following is not a mission of the PMC?

a. Steering the process toward quality objectives

b. Supporting and committing resources

c. Establishing personal performance bonuses

d. Resolving conflicts over objectives and resources

8. What is the Process Quality Team (PIT) responsible for?

a. Setting company-wide performance metrics

b. Implementing process management actions

c. Replacing the PMC when needed

d. Overseeing only the manufacturing process

9. Who typically heads the Process Quality Team (PIT)?

a. The functional owner

b. The focus owner

Practice Questions

c. The CEO

d. The general manager

10. What should the process owner ensure regarding information integrity?

a. That it exists throughout the process

b. That it is limited to financial data

c. That external auditors control it

d. That it is only used by top management

11. What is the primary goal of process ownership in LSS?

a. To create competition among departments

b. To tie personal goals to operational achievements

c. To manage the entire process and ensure its success

d. To reduce the workforce

12. How should the process owner be introduced to their responsibilities and authority?

a. Through a casual meeting

b. Via a formal announcement to all managers

c. By an informal email

d. By a peer manager

13. What is a critical success factor for the process owner?

a. Having a track record of defect-free results

b. Being a problem fixer

c. Focusing only on department goals

d. Limiting changes to the process

Practice Questions

14. What is the role of top management in supporting the process owner?
a. Approving resource allocation
b. Financing the process
c. Providing recognition for the owner
d. All of the above

15. What should be included in a process model?
a. Only the ideal state of the process
b. A detailed representation of the current process
c. Only graphical representations
d. Personal opinions of managers

16. What is an important aspect of the process owner's authority?
a. It should be kept secret from other managers
b. It must be clearly communicated to all concerned parties
c. It should only be known to the process owner
d. It should be limited to financial decisions

17. What does LSS seek to address through process ownership?
a. Narrow departmental focus
b. Increased competition among managers
c. Individual performance bonuses
d. Decreasing process efficiency

18. Who is responsible for resolving or escalating cross-functional issues?
a. The process owner
b. The CEO

Practice Questions

c. The department manager

d. The external consultant

19. What is the core principle of LSS regarding process management?

a. It should be independent of operating units

b. It should focus only on financial metrics

c. External auditors should control it

d. It should be limited to manufacturing processes

20. What should a process model avoid?

a. Describing the process as it currently exists

b. Including supporting textual documentation

c. Describing the process as it should be ideally

d. Using process flowcharts

21. What is the first step once ownership of a process has been established?

a. Implementing the process

b. Defining the mission and identifying the scope

c. Evaluating process performance

d. Training staff

22. What does the mission of a process describe?

a. The steps involved in the process

b. The technology used in the process

c. How the process helps to attain corporate goals

d. The cost of the process

Practice Questions

23. What should a mission statement be?

a. Lengthy and detailed

b. Concise and to the point

c. Written by external consultants

d. Focused primarily on cost

24. What does the scope of a business process define?

a. The technology used in the process

b. The exact cost of the process

c. The boundaries of the process

d. The number of employees involved

25. Which question is not one of the four required to define the scope of a process?

a. Where does the process start?

b. What does the process include?

c. Who is the process owner?

d. Where does the process end?

26. What might help in resolving disagreements over the scope of a process?

a. Identifying the process whose mission is most clearly related to the activity in question

b. Increasing the budget for the process

c. Firing team members who disagree

d. Ignoring the disagreements

27. Why is it important to specify what a process does not include?

a. To save costs

Practice Questions

b. To avoid making assumptions

c. To impress stakeholders

d. To simplify the process

28. When does the accounts receivable process begin?

a. When an invoice is issued and the accounts receivable system is updated

b. When the customer places an order

c. When the payment is received

d. When the product is delivered

29. What is one of the activities included in the accounts receivable process?

a. Manufacturing products

b. Collection or other settlement of customer accounts

c. Marketing and advertising

d. Hiring new staff

30. When does the accounts receivable process end?

a. When the customer places a new order

b. When the invoice is cleared and the accounts receivable system is updated

c. When the product is delivered

d. When the fiscal year ends

31. What does the procurement process cover?

a. Manufacturing of products

b. Purchasing "off the shelf" parts, equipment, or supplies from external suppliers

c. Marketing strategies

Practice Questions

d. Customer service activities

32. When does the procurement process begin?

a. When the supplier is chosen

b. When the requestor submits a purchase requisition

c. When the product is delivered

d. When the payment is made

33. What are critical success factors?

a. Areas where costs can be cut

b. Key areas of activity that must succeed for the process to achieve its goals

c. The number of employees involved in the process

d. The length of the process

34. Who should write the mission and scope of a process?

a. External consultants

b. The owner and the team

c. The customers and suppliers

d. The board of directors

35. Which of the following is not included in the scope of the accounts receivable process?

a. Accurate maintenance of customer accounts

b. Assessment of the creditworthiness of customers

c. Initiation and processing of credit notes

d. Manufacturing of products

Practice Questions

36. What might the preparation of regular reports in the accounts receivable process be used for?

a. Staff action

b. Marketing strategies

c. Product development

d. Hiring new staff

37. Which activity in the accounts receivable process involves notifying management?

a. Collection of customer accounts

b. Accurate maintenance of customer accounts

c. Notification to management of out-of-line situations

d. Assessment of the creditworthiness of customers

38. What is the purpose of monitoring the resolution of management directives in the accounts receivable process?

a. To ensure accurate maintenance of customer accounts

b. To assess the creditworthiness of customers

c. To ensure directives are followed correctly

d. To initiate credit notes

39. Which task is not typically part of the accounts receivable process?

a. Collection of customer accounts

b. Preparation of regular reports

c. Monitoring resolution of management directives

d. Designing new products

40. What shift in focus occurred in process improvement during the 1980s?

Practice Questions

a. From cost-cutting to quality improvement

b. From manufacturing processes to business process improvement

c. From customer service to product development

d. From marketing to recruitment

41. What are the five key process inputs in Lean Six Sigma?

a. Materials, machines, manpower, methods, and measurements

b. Materials, manpower, money, methods, and measurements

c. Machines, money, manpower, methods, and metrics

d. Machines, money, manpower, methods, and management

42. What is Lean accounting aligned within an organization?

a. Revenue streams

b. Cost centers

c. Value streams

d. Profit margins

43. What is the primary idea behind the Toyota Production System?

a. To increase the number of products produced

b. To maintain a continuous flow of products and adapt to demand changes

c. To reduce the workforce

d. To increase inventory levels

44. What is the purpose of the 5S methodology?

a. To increase sales

b. To organize, clean, develop, and sustain a productive work environment

c. To improve financial performance

Practice Questions

d. To reduce the number of employees

45. What does OEE stand for?
a. Overall Equipment Efficiency
b. Overall Equipment Effectiveness
c. Optimal Equipment Efficiency
d. Optimal Efficiency Evaluation

46. What is a Kanban?
a. A type of inventory system
b. A method of employee evaluation
c. A signal for employees to take action
d. A financial metric

47. What does Value Stream Mapping typically include?
a. Descriptions of the 5M's
b. Cost analysis of products
c. Inventory levels
d. Employee satisfaction surveys

48. Which of the following is a Lean tool used to reduce changeover times?
a. 5S
b. Kanban
c. SMED
d. TPM

49. What is the goal of Total Productive Maintenance (TPM)?

Practice Questions

a. To increase inventory levels

b. To minimize downtimes and maximize equipment usage

c. To reduce the number of employees

d. To increase the number of products produced

50. What is a key characteristic of a Lean operational philosophy?

a. It is a set of tools for process improvement only

b. It is embraced only by lower-level employees

c. It needs to be understood and embraced at the highest levels of the company

d. It focuses solely on financial performance

51. What is the primary objective of the Lean Six Sigma (LSS) practitioner?

a. To increase employee salaries

b. To identify and eliminate waste

c. To sell more products

d. To hire more employees

52. Which of the following is typically not considered a category of waste?

a. Overproduction

b. Excess inventory

c. Customer satisfaction

d. Defects

53. What kind of activity is described as something the external customer is willing to pay for?

a. No- Value Added (NVA) activity

b. Value Added (VA) activity

Practice Questions

c. Business Value Added (BVA) activity

d. Internal activity

54. What percentage of all organizational activities is estimated to be consumed by NVA activities?

a. 15%

b. 30%

c. 65%

d. 95%

55. Which concept refers to activities that are required to deliver your product or service to the customer?

a. No Value Added (NVA) activities

b. Value Added (VA) activities

c. Business Value Added (BVA) activities

d. Waste activities

56. What should be done if an activity does not appear to be something that the external customer would be willing to pay for?

a. Proceed with the activity

b. Question the activity

c. Increase the activity

d. Ignore the activity

57. What is a common term for activities that exist due to worst process design?

a. Value-added activities

b. Business-value-added activities

Practice Questions

c. Poor-quality cost

d. Strategic activities

58. What is the impact of communicating to key process personnel that their work is NVA?

a. It boosts morale

b. It destroys morale

c. It increases efficiency

d. It decreases waste

59. Why might it be a mistake to classify certain activities like safety and payroll as NVA?

a. It reduces operational costs

b. It increases customer satisfaction

c. It could destroy organizational morale

d. It enhances product quality

60. What does the ability to see something that others cannot refer to in Lean management?

a. Process improvement

b. Waste Identification

c. Employee training

d. Customer feedback

61. What is a common consequence of weak process control?

a. Improved customer satisfaction

b. Increased defects, rework, and high scrap rates

c. Decreased production costs

Practice Questions

d. Enhanced product quality

62. Why is poor equipment maintenance often a cause for defective products?

a. It increases production speed

b. It reduces the number of employees needed

c. It prevents equipment from breaking down

d. It leads to equipment breakdowns due to poor maintenance

63. What should be considered a defect?

a. Only what an employee can tangibly see in the product

b. Anything that contributes to a product not meeting customer expectations

c. Any product that passes quality control

d. Products that are too expensive to produce

64. What is processing waste?

a. Any effort that reduces the cost of production

b. Any effort that adds no value to the product or service from the customer's viewpoint

c. Any effort that increases the efficiency of the production process

d. Any effort that increases the quality of the product

65. What is a major source of processing waste in service industries?

a. Efficient order processing

b. Well-defined service-delivery requirements

c. Extensive processing waste from several apparent causes

d. Minimal information dissemination

Practice Questions

66. What must be done when a product or service is changed?

a. Nothing, continue with the existing process

b. Train personnel with new instructions

c. Increase production speed

d. Reduce the number of employees

67. What is just-in-case logic?

a. Producing only what is needed

b. Making more products just in case of unforeseen issues

c. Reducing inventory to cut costs

d. Implementing lean manufacturing principles

68. What happens when customer requirements are poorly understood?

a. Efficient production processes

b. Reduced processing waste

c. Extra processing occurs

d. Improved customer satisfaction

69. What is the result of overprocessing to accommodate downtime?

a. Increased production efficiency

b. Reduced overproduction and excess inventory

c. Overproduction and excess inventory

d. Improved employee morale

70. What is a typical communication cycle?

a. Sending emails within the organization

Practice Questions

b. Identifying CTQ customer requirements and transitioning them into product specifications

c. Ignoring customer requirements

d. Reducing the number of employees

71. What is the impact of redundant approvals?

a. Increased product cost and lead time

b. Improved efficiency

c. Reduced quality control

d. Enhanced customer satisfaction

72. How can excessive information sharing be a source of waste?

a. It reduces employee workload

b. It leads to information overload

c. It improves communication

d. It increases production speed

73. What is a common cause of waiting waste?

a. Efficient material conveyance

b. Well-maintained machinery

c. Materials conveyance delays

d. Balanced workloads

74. What is a prevalent root cause of waiting waste?

a. Efficient raw material management

b. Raw material outages

c. Balanced scheduling

d. Sufficient number of employees

Practice Questions

75. What can result from unbalanced workloads?

a. Efficient production processes

b. Waste of waiting

c. Reduced lead time

d. Improved product quality

76. What happens when there is unplanned downtime for maintenance?

a. Increased productivity

b. Waste of waiting

c. Reduced production costs

d. Improved machine efficiency

77. What is a primary source of waiting waste according to facility layout?

a. Properly sequenced equipment placement

b. Equipment placement based on open floor space

c. Efficient use of space

d. Reduced equipment downtime

78. What is the impact of long process setup times?

a. Increased productivity

b. Permanent loss of time to waiting

c. Reduced production costs

d. Improved product quality

79. What is a common misconception about automation?

a. Machines should always run to meet customer demand

Practice Questions

b. Machines should be used only when necessary

c. Automation reduces production waste

d. Automation increases employee workload

80. What should be the target for every process step?

a. 50% first-pass quality

b. 100% first-pass quality

c. Increased production speed

d. Reduced employee involvement

81. What is the ultimate objective of an LSS organization?

a. Increased production speed

b. Properly connecting materials, machines, manpower, and methods

c. Reducing the number of employees

d. Increased customer complaints

82. What can lead to the waste of motion?

a. Properly documented work methods

b. Consistent work methods

c. Inconsistent work methods

d. Efficient information management

83. How can poor information management contribute to waste?

a. By making required information available to employees

b. By reducing manual document transfers

c. By causing manual document transfers and information exchange delays

d. By improving communication efficiency

Practice Questions

84. What is a solution to inconsistent work methods?

a. Ignoring standard operating procedures

b. Creating standard operating procedures or visual work instructions

c. Increasing the number of employees

d. Reducing employee training

85. What is the result of the poor facility or cell layout?

a. Reduced waste of motion

b. Significant motion, transportation, and waiting wastes

c. Improved production speed

d. Enhanced employee satisfaction

86. What is a common source of the waste of motion in administrative areas?

a. Efficient document management

b. Manual transportation of documents

c. Reduced information exchange

d. Proper facility layout

87. What is a common cause of motion waste?

a. Efficient use of space

b. Proper training programs

c. Poor workplace organization and housekeeping

d. Well-documented work methods

88. How can employee interactions with materials and machinery result in motion waste?

a. By reducing the need for walking distances

Practice Questions

b. By increasing the need for hand delivery of materials

c. By improving production speed

d. By reducing employee workload

89. What is the effect of tribal knowledge in an organization?

a. Consistent work methods

b. Increased quality control

c. Inconsistent learning and practices

d. Improved employee training

90. What is a frequent result of poorly documented work methods?

a. Efficient production processes

b. Root cause of product or service quality issues

c. Reduced employee workload

d. Improved customer satisfaction

91. What is a common result of poor facility layout in a production environment?

a. Increased lead time

b. Decreased motion waste

c. Enhanced quality control

d. Reduced need for transportation equipment

92. What is the main objective of learning to see motion waste?

a. To increase employee training

b. To identify where and when motion waste occurs

c. To improve purchasing practices

d. To reduce the number of employees

Practice Questions

93. Transportation waste typically involves:

a. Only people

b. Only equipment

c. Both people and equipment

d. Neither people nor equipment

94. What is a major cause of transportation waste?

a. Small batch sizes

b. Poor purchasing practices

c. High employee turnover

d. Effective facility layout

95. What is the impact of poor purchasing practices on transportation waste?

a. It eliminates the need for transportation equipment

b. It leads to transportation waste and other types of waste

c. It reduces the cost of raw materials

d. It improves the quality of raw materials

96. What does an inadequate facility layout directly affect?

a. Employee satisfaction

b. Purchasing decisions

c. Productivity and profitability

d. Training programs

97. Which of the following is not a cause of transportation waste?

a. Poor purchasing practices

Practice Questions

b. Large batch sizes

c. Small storage areas

d. Inadequate facility layout

98. What is the primary goal of Lean Six Sigma practitioners?

a. To increase employee salaries

b. To understand process flow deeply

c. To reduce training costs

d. To maximize the number of employees

99. What does mapping product flows help with?

a. Reducing employee turnover

b. Visualizing processes that should be next to each other

c. Increasing transportation waste

d. Enhancing employee benefits

100. What is the waste of underutilized employees often caused by?

a. High investment in training

b. Low pay and high turnover strategy

c. Effective hiring practices

d. Well-defined job roles

101. What is a common trait of traditional organizations regarding employee pay?

a. High pay and low turnover rate

b. Low pay and high turnover rate

c. High pay and high turnover rate

d. Low pay and low turnover rate

Practice Questions

102. What does proper facility layout help reduce?

a. Employee training costs

b. Waste of waiting

c. Salaries

d. Company profits

103. How can behavior waste impact a company?

a. It has minimal impact

b. It can be extremely damaging

c. It only affects new employees

d. It only affects senior management

104. Which type of waste is characterized by employees not being used to their full potential?

a. Motion waste

b. Transportation waste

c. Underutilized employees waste

d. Overproduction waste

105. What is often the result of poor hiring practices?

a. High employee satisfaction

b. Matching skills to position requirements

c. Attracting and retaining skilled employees

d. Not getting the best candidate for the position

106. What is the relationship between training investment and company performance?

Practice Questions

a. Poor-performing companies invest heavily in training

b. Higher-performing companies tend to invest more in training

c. All companies invest the same amount in training

d. Training investment has no impact on company performance

107. What does the waste of motion checklist help identify?

a. Transportation waste

b. When and where motion waste occurs

c. Employee satisfaction levels

d. Product quality issues

108. What is a key characteristic of a low-pay, high-turnover strategy?

a. High employee morale

b. Low employee turnover

c. Poor working conditions

d. High investment in employee development

109. What does the term "value stream" refer to?

a. The supply chain of raw materials

b. The path across the organization that adds value for the customer

c. The flow of paperwork in the office

d. The hierarchy of management

110. What is the primary goal of value stream management?

a. To increase internal meetings

b. To focus on external customer response

c. To reduce the number of employees

Practice Questions

d. To increase inventory levels

111. What tool is often used to identify CTQ parameters?

a. Radar chart

b. Blue highlighter

c. Flowchart

d. Conflict resolution techniques

112. What is the goal of cycle time analysis and reduction?

a. Increase the time to move an item through a process

b. Reduce the time to move an item through a process

c. Add more steps to a process

d. Increase costs

113. What is one of the six worldwide best practices identified by the International Quality Study?

a. Increasing paperwork

b. Supplier certification

c. Adding more layers of approval

d. Delaying processes

114. Which of the following is not a typical way to reduce cycle time?

a. Doing activities in parallel

b. Changing activity sequence

c. Increasing interruptions

d. Reducing interruption

115. What is the impact of long cycle times on a business?

Practice Questions

a. Increased efficiency

b. Increased storage costs

c. Faster product delivery

d. Reduced costs

116. What was the result of Intel's bureaucracy elimination in terms of administrative steps for purchasing a ballpoint pen?

a. Increased to 95 steps

b. Reduced to 8 steps

c. Remained the same

d. Increased paperwork

117. What should be done before eliminating a bureaucratic activity?

a. Ignore its impact

b. Understand its purpose and impact

c. Increase checks and balances

d. Add more signatures

118. What is a common result of bureaucracy in organizations?

a. Increased efficiency

b. Increased delays

c. Reduced costs

d. Faster processes

119. What percentage of clerical work is typically spent on checking, filing, and retrieving information?

a. 10%

b. 40%

Practice Questions

c. 60%

d. 90%

120. What is a key objective in the attack on bureaucracy?

a. Increasing total cycle time

b. Financially justifying every approval signature

c. Adding more steps to the process

d. Ignoring cost-benefit analysis

121. What does "continuous flow" aim to achieve?

a. Maximizing the number of employees

b. Reducing the time products spend in storage

c. Making items one piece at a time

d. Increasing lead times

122. What does a "pull system" do?

a. Pushes products to the next stage regardless of demand

b. Replenishes materials based on customer demand

c. Increases inventory levels

d. Reduces product quality

123. What is "Point of Use Storage" (POUS)?

a. Storing materials far from the point of use

b. Locating materials at the point of value-adding activities

c. Centralizing all storage areas

d. Reducing the number of storage areas

Practice Questions

124. What is the concept of "quality at source"?

a. Inspecting quality after production

b. Building quality into processes as they are completed

c. Outsourcing quality control

d. Reducing quality control measures

125. What does "Takt time" represent?

a. The production rate of the factory

b. The break time for employees

c. The demand rate of the external customer

d. The lead time for raw materials

126. Which of the following is a primary requirement for successful Lean programs?

a. High employee turnover

b. Lean management concepts

c. High inventory levels

d. Low employee morale

127. What does the waste of transportation checklist help identify?

a. Employee training needs

b. Causes of transportation waste

c. Product defects

d. Production schedules

128. What does the term "muda" refer to in Lean terminology?

a. Value-added activities

b. Waste

Practice Questions

c. Customer satisfaction

d. Employee training

129. What is the primary cause of behavior waste?

a. Efficient workflows

b. Human interactions

c. Automated processes

d. High-quality materials

130. What can be a consequence of an employee's waste?

a. Increased productivity

b. Enhanced team collaboration

c. Restricted process improvement

d. Improved quality control

131. What are the two main types of techniques for waste identification in an LSS organization?

a. Quantitative and Qualitative

b. Visual and Analytical

c. Manual and Automated

d. Internal and External

132. What is the primary fundamental strength of the Lean portion of LSS?

a. Quantitative data analysis

b. Qualitative techniques

c. Automated processes

d. High-speed production

Practice Questions

133. What concept is used to describe storing materials and tools where they are used by value-adding employees?

a. Just-in-Time

b. Kaizen

c. Point of Use Storage

d. Pull Systems

134. What is value stream management primarily concerned with?

a. Managing inventory levels

b. Visualizing the value stream

c. Conducting quality inspections

d. Managing all aspects of value creation for the customer

135. Which waste does the concept of continuous flow aim to eliminate?

a. Excess inventory

b. Waiting

c. Overproduction

d. Defective products

136. In a service industry, the value stream is more likely to be composed of:

a. Materials and equipment

b. Information management, documentation management, or activity management

c. Manufacturing processes

d. Raw materials inventory

137. What is a key challenge in identifying the value stream in a government agency?

Practice Questions

a. Lack of resources

b. Multiple stakeholders with different views of value

c. Poor-quality materials

d. Inconsistent customer demand

138. Which tool is often used to achieve quality at the source?

a. Just-in-Time

b. Value stream mapping

c. Mistake proofing

d. Pull systems

139. What does the term "Kaizen" mean?

a. Change for the better

b. Inventory management

c. Quality at the source

d. Customer satisfaction

140. What are the 5M's in Lean Six Sigma?

a. Materials, Machines, Manpower, Methods, and Measurements

b. Metrics, Models, Manpower, Methods, and Machines

c. Materials, Machines, Metrics, Methods, and Management

d. Measurements, Methods, Manpower, Machines, and Maintenance

141. Which of the following tools is most appropriate for identifying potential causes of a process issue?

a. Control Chart

b. Fishbone Diagram

c. Histogram

Practice Questions

d. Pareto Chart

142. Which concept ensures resources are not expended until customer demand is placed?

a. Just-in-Time

b. Continuous flow

c. Pull systems

d. Quality at the source

143. What is an integral part of any new process or process revision in Lean?

a. Inventory management

b. Quality at the source

c. Just-in-Time

d. Continuous flow

144. What is the ultimate objective of Just-in-Time (JIT)?

a. Maximizing inventory levels

b. Minimizing material costs

c. Minimizing inventory carrying costs

d. Maximizing production speed

145. Which waste is most commonly introduced by poor quality of information?

a. Overproduction

b. Waiting

c. Transportation

d. All nine wastes

Practice Questions

146. What does the value stream include in an organization?

a. Only materials and manpower

b. VA and NVA waste activities

c. Only value-adding processes

d. Only customer interactions

147. How is the value stream visualized in LSS?

a. Through customer feedback

b. Through value stream mapping

c. Through quality inspections

d. Through financial analysis

148. What is required for a successful waste elimination plan?

a. High-speed production

b. Advanced machinery

c. Effective waste identification and Lean concept/tool selection

d. Large inventory

149. What is a common business measure related to JIT?

a. Defect rates

b. Inventory turns

c. Employee productivity

d. Customer satisfaction

150. What is the primary focus of quality at the source?

a. Inspecting final products

b. Minimizing production speed

Practice Questions

c. Producing quality at each individual VA step

d. Reducing inventory levels

151. Which of the following is an example of qualitative waste identification?

a. Statistical process control

b. Identifying waste through POUS

c. Measuring cycle times

d. Calculating defect rates

152. What does continuous flow help to reduce?

a. Material costs

b. Lead time

c. Employee training time

d. Product variety

153. Which of the following is not a component of value stream management?

a. Vendor relationships

b. Operational philosophy

c. Financial auditing

d. Performance measurement

154. Which organization has successfully applied value stream management in recent years?

a. Federal Reserve

b. Navy

c. World Health Organization

d. International Red Cross

Practice Questions

155. Which Six Sigma tool is primarily used to determine the relative importance of different inputs to a process?

a. Control Chart

b. SIPOC Diagram

c. Design of Experiments (DOE)

d. Pareto Chart

156. What activity is central to the role of a Lean practitioner?

a. Conducting financial audits

b. Managing inventory

c. Understanding all value stream components

d. Designing new products

157. What does the concept of flow aim to link seamlessly?

a. Inventory orders

b. All VA steps

c. Management levels

d. Customer feedback

158. In Lean Six Sigma, what are KPIVs?

a. Key Process Input Variables

b. Key Product Inspection Variables

c. Key Performance Indicator Variables

d. Key Production Improvement Variables

159. What is the primary purpose of value stream mapping?

a. To measure employee productivity

Practice Questions

b. To visualize the entire value stream

c. To calculate production costs

d. To assess financial performance

160. Which Lean concept is described as the "Holy Grail" in manufacturing or service delivery?

a. Just-in-Time

b. Quality at the source

c. Continuous flow

d. Kaizen

161. What is the primary target of organizational process improvement programs?

a. Increase employee salaries

b. More effective use of resources

c. Increase marketing budget

d. Expand office space

162. Which of the following techniques is commonly used in the Control phase to ensure process consistency?

a. Kaizen

b. Statistical Process Control (SPC)

c. Root Cause Analysis

d. Fishbone Diagram

163. What is the purpose of 5S Workplace Organization and Standardization?

a. Increase employee vacation time

Practice Questions

b. Organize housekeeping activities and standardize materials, machinery, manpower, and methodologies

c. Improve customer relations

d. Enhance digital marketing strategies

164. Which phase of 5S involves eliminating anything that is not needed?

a. Sort

b. Set-in-order

c. Shine

d. Standardize

165. What is the primary objective of the 'Shine' phase in 5S?

a. Increase sales

b. Ensure the entire area is completely clean

c. Create new products

d. Hire new employees

166. In the context of 5S, what does 'sustain' mean?

a. Developing the discipline to maintain the 5S program

b. Increasing profits

c. Reducing employee hours

d. Changing the company logo

167. What is a common mistake organizations make when implementing KPOVs?

a. Focusing too much on externally focused measures

b. Having too many internally focused measures

c. Ignoring customer needs

Practice Questions

d. Implementing too many Lean tools

168. Which of the following statistical tools is often used in the Analyze phase to identify relationships between variables?

a. Control Charts

b. Correlation Coefficient

c. Scatter Plots

d. Histogram

169. Which of the following is not one of the three direct measurements of OEE?

a. Equipment availability

b. Equipment performance

c. Product Quality

d. Employee satisfaction

170. What is the primary purpose of mistake-proofing?

a. Increase sales

b. Minimize or eliminate mistakes

c. Hire more employees

d. Enhance digital marketing

171. Which cycle is typically used in mistake proofing?

a. PDCA cycle

b. DMAIC cycle

c. SDLC cycle

d. Waterfall cycle

Practice Questions

172. What is the primary goal of cellular manufacturing?

a. Organize VA activities into the most effective and least resource-consuming series of activities

b. Increase employee salaries

c. Enhance digital marketing

d. Reduce the number of employees

173. What is the first step in creating manufacturing cells?

a. Chart the current work sequence

b. Measure demand

c. Group products

d. Combine work and balance process

174. Which phase in 5S is the most challenging for organizations to maintain?

a. Sort

b. Set-in-order

c. Shine

d. Standardize

175. Which Lean tool is used to make visible the requirement for action on the part of employees?

a. 5S

b. OEE

c. Kanban

d. Value Stream Mapping

176. What does Kanban mean in Japanese?

Practice Questions

a. Signal

b. Card

c. Work

d. Flow

177. What is the primary benefit of using Kanban in a process?

a. Increase employee salaries

b. Produce only what the customer requested

c. Enhance digital marketing

d. Hire more employees

178. What is the first step in Value Stream Mapping (VSM)?

a. Create a future state map

b. Identify customer needs

c. Construct a current state map

d. Eliminate waste

179. Why is the future state map important in VSM?

a. It defines and outlines how you want your organization to perform in the future

b. It identifies current weaknesses

c. It lists customer complaints

d. It increases employee salaries

180. Which of the following is not a phase in the 5S program?

a. Sort

b. Shine

c. Standardize

Practice Questions

d. Supervise

181. What is the primary purpose of creating a cell in cellular manufacturing?

a. Simplify material flow

b. Hire more employees

c. Increase sales

d. Reduce employee hours

182. What is a common tool used to sustain the 5S program?

a. Cleaning schedules

b. Marketing strategies

c. Hiring policies

d. Salary increments

183. What is the purpose of a red tag in the 'Sort' phase of 5S?

a. Identify items that are needed

b. Identify items that are wanted but not needed

c. Increase sales

d. Enhance digital marketing

184. What is the primary focus of Lean tools?

a. Increase marketing budget

b. Improve productivity

c. Increase employee salaries

d. Enhance digital marketing

185. Which of the following is not a key step in the successful design and implementation of a manufacturing cell?

Practice Questions

a. Group products

b. Measure demand

c. Combine work and balance process

d. Increase marketing budget

186. What is the main objective of the 'Set-in-order' phase in 5S?

a. To set items in order of use

b. Increase sales

c. Hire more employees

d. Enhance digital marketing

187. What does VA stand for in the context of Lean Six Sigma?

a. Value-Added

b. Virtual Assistance

c. Variable Adjustment

d. Visual Aid

188. What is one key benefit of implementing an effective 5S program?

a. Increase employee salaries

b. Create a safe, neat, orderly workplace

c. Enhance digital marketing

d. Hire more employees

189. What is a critical component of the 'Shine' phase in 5S?

a. Clean and sweep the entire area

b. Hire more employees

c. Increase sales

Practice Questions

d. Enhance digital marketing

190. Why is it important to use standardized tools in the 'Standardize' phase of 5S?

a. To maintain a consistent application of 5S activities

b. Increase marketing budget

c. Hire more employees

d. Enhance digital marketing

191. What is one of the critical factors for the success of an LSS project?

a. Employee satisfaction

b. Understanding the nature of the measurement system

c. Financial investment

d. Market research

192. What type of measures should be considered when formulating an LSS project?

a. Employee satisfaction measures

b. Financial Measures

c. Department measures

d. Technological measures

193. Which of the following is not a type of measure that can influence resistance to change in an LSS project?

a. Individual employee performance measures

b. Customer-related performance measures

c. Technological innovation measures

d. Regulatory agency measures

Practice Questions

194. What is a fundamental characteristic of operating in an LSS environment?

a. High financial investment

b. Challenging current beliefs and practices

c. Hiring new employees

d. Outsourcing tasks

195. What is the first step in rewriting beliefs to transition to an LSS environment?

a. Implementing new technology

b. Letting go of old beliefs

c. Increasing employee salaries

d. Conducting market research

196. What is the second phase in successfully transitioning to a new set of beliefs and behaviors in an LSS environment?

a. Implementing new policies

b. Conducting performance reviews

c. Opening up the mind to new ways of thinking

d. Hiring new management

197. What should employees question on a daily basis in an LSS environment?

a. Their salary

b. The activities they conduct and whether they create value for the customer

c. The company's financial performance

d. The technological advancements in the industry

Practice Questions

198. Which of the following is a common method for determining whether a process improvement is statistically significant?

a. Pareto Analysis

b. Hypothesis Testing

c. SIPOC Diagram

d. Value Stream Mapping

199. What does the term "Kaikaku" refer to?

a. Small, continuous improvements

b. Radical changes

c. Employee training programs

d. Financial audits

200. What is the essence of considering new possibilities in an LSS environment?

a. Adopting new technology

b. Developing a learning environment

c. Increasing market share

d. Conducting financial audits

201. What is essential for the emergence of an LSS environment?

a. High employee turnover

b. Continued practice of leaving old beliefs behind and considering new possibilities

c. Increased financial investment

d. Hiring external consultants

Practice Questions

202. What is the first step of Kaizen for process troubleshooting?

a. Finding the root cause

b. Taking temporary countermeasures

c. Conducting Gembutsu

d. Going to Gemba

203. What should be done during the "Do" phase of the PDCA cycle?

a. Establish a target for improvement

b. Implement the plan

c. Determine whether implementation has brought planned improvement

d. Standardize the new procedures

204. Which of the following is not one of the four K's of Kaizen?

a. Kusai

b. Kitsui

c. Kakushin

d. Kiken

205. What is the role of management in a Lean organization?

a. Maintenance and improvement

b. Financial management

c. Marketing and sales

d. Outsourcing tasks

206. Which step in Kaizen for process troubleshooting involves assessing all relevant information surrounding the problem?

a. Step 1: Go to Gemba

b. Step 2: Conduct Gembutsu

Practice Questions

c. Step 3: Take temporary countermeasures

d. Step 4: Find root causes

207. What should be done to prevent the recurrence of a problem in Kaizen for process troubleshooting?

a. Implement temporary measures

b. Find root causes

c. Standardize the use of the new procedure

d. Conduct financial audits

208. What is the benefit of using Kaizen teams?

a. Increased financial investment

b. Cross-functional collaboration for process improvement

c. Reduced employee workload

d. Outsourcing tasks

209. How should management prepare for a Kaizen event?

a. Select target area

b. Increase employee salaries

c. Hire external consultants

d. Conduct market research

210. What is the role of an external consultant in a Kaizen event?

a. Increase financial investment

b. Mentor team members and provide objective insights

c. Conduct market research

d. Implement new technology

Practice Questions

211. What is one of the main obstacles during Kaizen?

a. High financial investment

b. The "we can't" syndrome

c. Lack of new technology

d. Market competition

212. What is a common mistake made by organizations during Kaizen for process troubleshooting?

a. Finding root causes

b. Implementing temporary measures only

c. Conducting market research

d. Hiring new employees

213. What should be the focus of Kaizen teams?

a. Financial performance

b. Process improvement

c. Market share

d. Technological innovation

214. What is the essence of Lean management in an LSS environment?

a. Financial management

b. Development of new processes

c. Marketing and sales

d. Outsourcing tasks

215. What is the role of employees in Kaizen?

a. Participate and share ideas

b. Conduct financial audits

Practice Questions

c. Implement new technology

d. Increase market share

216. What should be done during the "Check" phase of the PDCA cycle?

a. Plan for improvement

b. Implement the plan

c. Determine whether implementation has brought planned improvement

d. Standardize the new procedures

217. What is the purpose of the "Act" phase in the PDCA cycle?

a. Plan for improvement

b. Implement the plan

c. Determine whether implementation has brought planned improvement

d. Standardize the new procedures

218. What is a critical step in Kaizen for process troubleshooting to avoid recurring problems?

a. Implement temporary measures

b. Conduct market research

c. Standardize the new procedures

d. Increase financial investment

219. What should be done if Kaizen events fail to achieve anticipated results?

a. Conduct financial audits

b. Revise preparation and focus

c. Hire new employees

d. Increase market share

Practice Questions

220. What is one of the key benefits of conducting Kaizen events with cross-functional teams?

a. Increased financial benefit

b. Enhanced idea generation and creativity

c. Reduced employee workload

d. Market research opportunities

221. What does the phrase "beliefs drive behavior" imply in the context of Lean Six Sigma (LSS)?

a. Behavior is independent of beliefs.

b. Beliefs are influenced by external factors.

c. Beliefs determine how employees act and respond.

d. Behavior influences beliefs.

222. What should managers do when faced with the employee response "we can't"?

a. Accept the response and move on.

b. Challenge the response by exploring what could be done if the change were possible.

c. Ignore the employee's response.

d. Replace the employee.

223. What is the recommended action if a Kaizen event doesn't work?

a. Abandon Kaizen.

b. Repeat the Kaizen process.

c. Try a different methodology.

d. Blame the employees.

Practice Questions

224. What does Kaikaku mean?

a. Small incremental changes.

b. Radical transformation or innovation.

c. Maintaining the status quo.

d. A temporary fix.

225. Which of the following is not an attribute of Kaizen?

a. Involves everyone in the organization.

b. Focuses on results rather than processes.

c. Puts quality first all the time.

d. Defines the "next process" as the customer.

226. What is the misconception of management in most Western companies regarding Lean?

a. Lean is a long-term commitment.

b. Lean is just a set of tools.

c. Lean requires a transformation of mind.

d. Lean is customer-focused.

227. What does a true Lean facility layout require?

a. A lot of space.

b. Traditional equipment placement.

c. Consideration of customer demand.

d. Ignoring employee input.

228. What is the primary focus when considering a new facility layout?

a. Cost reduction.

b. Customer demand.

Practice Questions

c. Employee convenience.

d. Aesthetic appearance.

229. What is the purpose of a "walk-through" Lean layout?

a. To finalize the layout design.

b. To visualize and test the layout before implementation.

c. To train employees.

d. To impress clients.

230. What does Kakushin mean in the context of Lean?

a. Small changes.

b. Radical transformation.

c. Innovation.

d. Maintenance.

231. What is the new strategic mantra for corporations?

a. Cost-cutting.

b. Revenue growth.

c. Employee satisfaction.

d. Market stability.

232. How many essentials are there in the 20-20 innovation process?

a. Four.

b. Five.

c. Six.

d. Seven.

Practice Questions

233. Which essential of the 20-20 innovation process involves creating a strategy for various alternative points of view?

a. Generate the mindset.

b. Know the territory.

c. Build the relationships.

d. Manage the journeys.

234. What is the primary skill required in the "Know the territory" stage of the 20-20 innovation process?

a. Building relationships.

b. Acquiring strategic knowledge.

c. Managing projects.

d. Implementing solutions.

235. What is the focus of the "Build the relationships" stage in the 20-20 innovation process?

a. Creating a strategy.

b. Cultivating quality communications and interaction.

c. Implementing solutions.

d. Managing projects.

236. What does the "Manage the journeys" stage concentrate on?

a. Identifying opportunities.

b. Building relationships.

c. Choosing projects and defining strategies.

d. Implementing solutions.

Practice Questions

237. What is the role of the "Create the solutions" stage in the 20-20 innovation process?

a. Building relationships.

b. Managing projects.

c. Designing end-to-end solutions.

d. Acquiring strategic knowledge.

238. Which personality is associated with the "Generate the mindset" essential?

a. Discoverer.

b. Innovator.

c. Communicator.

d. Performer.

239. Who is likely to be a "Discoverer" in the 20-20 innovation process?

a. Engineer.

b. Politician.

c. Historian.

d. Entertainer.

240. What is the primary focus of the "Deliver the results" stage?

a. Cultivating relationships.

b. Implementing effective solutions.

c. Generating ideas.

d. Acquiring knowledge.

241. Which essential involves transforming problems into opportunities using an IQ assessment?

Practice Questions

a. Generate the mindset.

b. Know the territory.

c. Build the relationships.

d. Manage the journeys.

242. What is the purpose of the Knowledge Wizard® software?

a. To build relationships.

b. To acquire the right information about the environment.

c. To implement solutions.

d. To create a strategy.

243. What is the main activity in the "Create the solutions" stage?

a. Building loyalty.

b. Managing journeys.

c. Designing comprehensive solutions.

d. Acquiring knowledge.

244. Which personality is associated with building loyalty and trust?

a. Innovator.

b. Communicator.

c. Performer.

d. Discoverer.

245. What is the outcome of a successful Kaikaku?

a. Incremental changes.

b. Radical transformation of mind and practices.

c. Maintaining the status quo.

d. Temporary improvements.

246. What is the role of the "Innovator" in the 20-20 innovation process?

a. Acquiring knowledge.

b. Building relationships.

c. Generating ideas and strategies.

d. Implementing solutions.

247. What should be considered when designing a Lean facility layout?

a. Employee preferences.

b. Traditional methods.

c. Customer demand and flow of materials.

d. Latest technology.

248. What is the significance of customer demand in Lean principles?

a. It is secondary to employee convenience.

b. It drives the organization's processes and layout.

c. It is less important than cost reduction.

d. It should be ignored in initial planning.

249. In the context of Lean, what does the term "POUS" stand for?

a. Point of Use Storage.

b. Plan of Universal Strategy.

c. Process of Utilizing Storage.

d. Point of Ultimate Strategy.

250. What is a major consideration in creating a mixed-model pull system?

Practice Questions

a. Employee preferences.

b. Inventory control.

c. Traditional job roles.

d. Aesthetic design.

251. What is the focus of the 'Playmakers' in the context of organizational change?

a. Setting goals

b. Asking about alternatives and eliminations

c. Executing strategies

d. Managing resources

252. What is the first component of managing journeys in the context of organizational change?

a. Define success

b. Solve the right problems at the right time

c. Choose destinations and set directions

d. Plan for the unexpected

253. Which methodology is mentioned for revealing and solving problems in the solution creation phase?

a. DMAIC

b. DMADV

c. PDSA

d. PDCA

254. In the solution creation phase, what is the key to moving from team to capability?

Practice Questions

a. Finding the right people

b. Getting the right tools to do the job

c. Learning to conserve resources

d. Designing solutions that evolve

255. Which phase involves moving from power to sustainable advantage?

a. Creating the solutions

b. Deliver the results

c. Managing the journeys

d. Kaikaku

256. What does the Knowledge Wizard emphasize in the delivery results phase?

a. Strategy formulation

b. Resource allocation

c. Intuitive, disciplined execution

d. Innovation

257. What is not mentioned as a component of the sixth phase of delivering results?

a. Simplify and specify

b. Set the pace and pilot the course

c. Design, build, and maintain optimal solutions

d. Optimize risk and return

258. What is one of the three primary obstacles to effective LSS process improvements?

a. Lack of resources

Practice Questions

b. Fear of the unknown

c. Poor leadership

d. Inadequate tools

259. What is Kaizen primarily associated within the context of change?

a. Large-scale transformations

b. Small process improvement projects

c. Financial planning

d. Marketing strategies

260. How long can Kaizen team activities typically last?

a. A few hours

b. 2 to 4 days or several weeks

c. One month

d. Several months

261. What concept reflects the LSS practitioners' advanced knowledge?

a. Kaizen

b. Kaikaku

c. Transformation of mind

d. Kakushin

262. The transformation of mind concept allows practitioners to think and act across what?

a. Individual tasks

b. The entire value stream

c. Financial metrics

d. Marketing strategies

Practice Questions

263. What is the third fundamental concept for systematic change by innovation?

a. Kaizen events

b. Transformation of mind

c. Standardized approach to change

d. Employee engagement

264. Which innovation process demonstrates the six essentials of innovation?

a. 20-20 innovation process

b. 10-10 innovation process

c. Kaizen process

d. Six Sigma process

265. Your Six Sigma team has identified a significant variance in the delivery times of products to customers. During the Analyze phase, you want to determine whether the variance is due to special causes or common causes. What tool would be most effective for this analysis?

a. Scatter Plot

b. Control Chart

c. Histogram

d. Fishbone Diagram

266. Which of the following is not an essential innovation in the 20-20 process?

a. Create the solutions

b. Deliver the results

c. Execute the strategy

d. Manage the journeys

267. What does the 'Create the solutions' stage involve?

a. Planning project timelines

b. Designing, building, and maintaining optimal solutions

c. Setting financial goals

d. Hiring new employees

268. In the context of LSS, what does DMADV stand for?

a. Define, Measure, Analyze, Design, Verify

b. Define, Measure, Assess, Design, Verify

c. Design, Measure, Analyze, Develop, Verify

d. Design, Measure, Assess, Develop, Verify

269. What should organizations learn to do to win big later on, according to the delivery results phase?

a. Fail small and early

b. Invest heavily upfront

c. Delay decision-making

d. Focus solely on short-term gains

270. What are employees expected to systematically eliminate by deploying change management concepts?

a. Innovation

b. Financial resources

c. Waste

d. Customer interactions

Practice Questions

271. What is a key question to ask in the solution creation phase about the people involved?

a. Do we have the right people and capability skill sets behind it?

b. Are the employees satisfied with their roles?

c. Do we have enough financial resources?

d. Are we meeting customer expectations?

272. What is crucial to get to the right people in the solution creation phase?

a. Financial resources

b. Market data

c. Right information

d. Customer feedback

273. What does the 'Deliver the results' stage concentrate on?

a. Creating new strategies

b. Sustainable advantage through implementation

c. Hiring new talent

d. Resource allocation

274. What is one of the elements of disciplined execution in the delivery results phase?

a. Setting unattainable goals

b. Intuitive execution

c. Simplifying processes

d. Delaying tasks

275. What is a component of the fifth phase of creating solutions?

a. Optimize risk and return

Practice Questions

b. Learn to fail small and early

c. Design, build, and maintain optimal solutions using DMADV

d. Maintain your leading cutting edge

276. What is the purpose of setting the pace and piloting the course in the delivery results phase?

a. To control financial expenditures

b. To ensure timely and effective execution

c. To increase employee satisfaction

d. To reduce resource usage

277. What is the main objective of Kaizen teams?

a. Financial planning

b. Marketing strategies

c. Larger scope process improvement projects

d. Individual task management

278. What does the 'manage the journeys' phase include?

a. Financial planning

b. Solving the right problems at the right time

c. Hiring new employees

d. Marketing strategies

279. What should organizations plan for in the journey management phase?

a. Financial stability

b. Unexpected events

c. Market Expansion

d. Employee training

Practice Questions

280. You are leading a project to reduce defects in a manufacturing process. During the Measure phase, you find that the current process capability (Cp) is below the desired level. What should be your next step?

a. Implement a new process without further analysis

b. Conduct a root cause analysis to identify the factors affecting process capability

c. Immediately proceed to the Improve phase

d. Redefine the project scope and goals

281. Who originated the term Six Sigma?

a. William J. Weisz

b. Bill Smith

c. Phil Crosby

d. Henry Ford Sr.

282. What was the standard of performance for Six Sigma according to Motorola?

a. 66.8 defects per million opportunities

b. 2.0 defects per million opportunities

c. Zero defects

d. 3.4 defects per million opportunities

283. What is the long-term process capability target set by Motorola?

a. Cp = 2.0

b. Cpk = 1.5

c. Cp = 1.0

d. Cpk = 2.0

Practice Questions

284. What does the term 'Six Sigma' statistically refer to?

a. Plus or minus three sigma

b. Zero defects

c. Plus or minus Six Sigma

d. Plus or minus two sigma

285. Who is known for setting the standard of performance in control charts as plus or minus three sigma?

a. William J. Weisz

b. Bill Smith

c. Shewhart

d. Phil Crosby

286. Which methodology did Motorola use to implement Six Sigma concepts?

a. PDCA cycle

b. Lean manufacturing

c. Kaizen

d. Kanban

287. What was the modified version of Shewhart's PDCA cycle called by Dr. Mikel Harry from Motorola?

a. DMAIC

b. DMADV

c. RDMAICSI

d. PDCA+

Practice Questions

288. Which concept focuses on reducing variation around the midpoint of a specification?

a. Lean

b. Six Sigma

c. Kaizen

d. Kanban

289. What does SSBB stand for?

a. Six Sigma Black Belt

b. Six Sigma Blue Belt

c. Six Sigma Bronze Belt

d. Six Sigma Business Belt

290. What should be the minimum savings generated by an SSBB per year as a result of their direct activities?

a. USD $100,000

b. USD $500,000

c. USD $1 million

d. USD $2 million

291. What percentage of time does an SSBB spend teaching either formally or informally?

a. 35%

b. 20%

c. 15%

d. 10%

292. Which skill is not listed as a requirement for an SSBB?

Practice Questions

a. Project management

b. Leadership

c. Adult learning

d. Software development

293. How long is the typical SSBB assignment?

a. 1 year

b. 2 years

c. 3 years

d. 4 years

294. What is the recommended number of SSBBs for every 100 employees?

a. 1 SSBB

b. 2 SSBBs

c. 3 SSBBs

d. 4 SSBBs

295. Which belt level is considered the first level in Six Sigma training?

a. Six Sigma Green Belt

b. Six Sigma Black Belt

c. Six Sigma Yellow Belt

d. Six Sigma Master Black Belt

296. What does DMAIC stand for?

a. Define, Measure, Analyze, Improve, Control

b. Design, Measure, Analyze, Design, Verify

c. Define, Measure, Act, Improve, Control

Practice Questions

d. Design, Measure, Act, Improve, Control

297. You have completed the Analyze phase of your Six Sigma project and identified several root causes for defects. Some team members suggest addressing all root causes simultaneously. What is your best course of action?

a. Address all root causes at once to maximize impact

b. Prioritize root causes based on their impact and feasibility

c. Focus only on the most obvious root cause

d. Present all root causes to management for further direction

298. Who further refined Lean concepts to develop the most effective auto assembly process in the world?

a. Henry Ford Sr.

b. William J. Weisz

c. Bill Smith

d. Toyota

299. Your Six Sigma project involves reducing cycle time in a service process. After mapping the process, you find several non-value-added steps. What should you do next?

a. Eliminate all non-value-added steps immediately

b. Analyze the necessity of each non-value-added step

c. Document the findings and move to the Control phase

d. Consult with upper management before making changes

300. What is the objective of the DMADV methodology?

a. To improve existing processes

b. To design new processes

Practice Questions

c. To control existing processes

d. To measure existing processes

301. What is the primary benefit of benchmarking for an organization?

a. Reduced working hours

b. Improved customer satisfaction

c. Increased product prices

d. Decreased employee engagement

302. Which of the following is not a type of benchmarking?

a. Internal

b. External

c. Mixed

d. Comprehensive

303. During which decade did IBM realize the benefits of adopting the best existing practices worldwide?

a. 1950s

b. 1960s

c. 1970s

d. 1980s

304. What significant discovery did Xerox make in the late 1970s regarding its Japanese affiliate, Fuji-Xerox?

a. Fuji-Xerox had higher-quality products.

b. Fuji-Xerox was selling copiers at manufacturing cost.

c. Fuji-Xerox had better customer service.

d. Fuji-Xerox had more advanced technology.

Practice Questions

305. Which company cites benchmarking as a major tool powering its improvement process and won the Malcolm Baldrige Award in 1988?

a. IBM

b. Xerox

c. Motorola

d. General Electric

306. What is the first step in an internal benchmarking effort?

a. Develop benchmark measurements

b. Select locations

c. Identify what to benchmark

d. Conduct location visits

307. What should be done after exchanging data in the internal benchmarking process?

a. Conduct telephone interviews and surveys

b. Implement changes

c. Develop a database

d. Select locations

308. In external benchmarking, what is the term for investigating a competitor's products, services, and processes?

a. Process analysis

b. Reverse engineering

c. Competitive analysis

d. Comparative review

Practice Questions

309. What is the primary reason for using process benchmarking?

a. To reduce costs

b. For goal setting and process development

c. To increase sales

d. To restructure the organization

310. What is one of the most common ways to collect information on external organizations?

a. Internal surveys

b. Literature searches

c. Employee interviews

d. Customer feedback

311. Which phase involves the improvement of the item's performance in the combined benchmarking process?

a. Phase I

b. Phase II

c. Phase IV

d. Phase V

312. Which method is commonly used to measure changes in the benchmarking process?

a. Ratio measurements

b. Qualitative assessments

c. Visual inspections

d. Customer surveys

Practice Questions

313. In external benchmarking, what is the term for benchmarking against non-competitive world-class organizations?

a. Competitive benchmarking

b. Functional benchmarking

c. World-class operations benchmarking

d. Activity-type benchmarking

314. What should be developed after collecting and analyzing internal data?

a. Implementation plan

b. Benchmarking committee

c. Benchmark database

d. Data collection plan

315. Which company realized a significant international competitive advantage by adopting best practices in the 1960s?

a. Motorola

b. IBM

c. General Electric

d. Xerox

316. What should be done immediately after a site visit in the external benchmarking process?

a. Conduct follow-up surveys

b. Update the benchmark database

c. Hold a team meeting to consolidate observations

d. Contact management

317. What is an essential ingredient in becoming and staying world class?

Practice Questions

a. Qualitative data

b. Strong leadership

c. Quantitative data

d. Customer loyalty

318. What is a key activity in Phase II of the combined benchmarking process?

a. Collect external original research information

b. Conduct internal site visits

c. Develop the data collection plan

d. Identify corrective actions

319. Which form of benchmarking extends to involve dissimilar industries?

a. Activity-type benchmarking

b. World-class operations benchmarking

c. Functional benchmarking

d. Competitive benchmarking

320. What should be established to measure the impact of changes in the benchmarking process?

a. Benchmarking committee

b. Measurement system

c. Ratio analysis

d. Process map

321. What is the main focus of process benchmarking?

a. Identifying new markets

b. Improving product quality

Practice Questions

c. Discovering methods for process improvement

d. Reducing operational costs

322. What is the primary goal of conducting a change-impact analysis in benchmarking?

a. To increase employee satisfaction

b. To improve customer relations

c. To prioritize implementation activities

d. To develop new products

323. Which organization is recommended to be used for developing an initial list of target trade and professional associations?

a. Encyclopedia of Trade Associations

b. International Trade Bureau

c. Global Benchmarking Network

d. World Trade Organization

324. What is a common characteristic to consider when selecting organizations for external benchmarking?

a. Size of the organization

b. Type of industry

c. Location of headquarters

d. Number of employees

325. What is an example of an effort-related process measurement?

a. Product dimensions

b. Cost per unit

c. Customer satisfaction score

Practice Questions

d. Delivery time

326. Your team has successfully implemented a solution to reduce defects in a production line. However, during the Control phase, you notice that the improvements are not being maintained. What is the best action to take?

a. Revise the project charter

b. Increase monitoring and measurement of key metrics

c. Conduct another round of training for all employees

d. Change the team responsible for the process

327. What should be done before generating data for process benchmarking?

a. Select benchmarking sites

b. Understand the product, process, or activity to be benchmarked

c. Develop an implementation plan

d. Contact trade associations

328. What kinds of data are crucial for managing and controlling processes in benchmarking?

a. Qualitative data

b. Historical data

c. Quantitative data

d. Predictive data

329. What is the primary advantage of using ratio measurements in benchmarking?

a. They provide absolute values.

b. They are easier to calculate.

c. They allow data exchange without disclosing sensitive information.

Practice Questions

d. They are specific to product types.

330. What is the crucial step after identifying what to benchmark in the internal benchmarking process?

a. Conducting site visits

b. Reviewing plans with experts

c. Obtaining management support

d. Exchanging data

331. What is the primary goal of bureaucracy elimination?

a. Increase paperwork

b. Enhance efficiency and effectiveness

c. Create more rules

d. Delay processes

332. What does streamlining imply?

a. Increased bureaucracy

b. Symmetry and beauty of design

c. More paperwork

d. Additional layers of approval

333. Which approach involves flowcharting a process to identify bureaucracy?

a. Incident-focused approach

b. Process-focused approach

c. Conflict resolution

d. Cycle time analysis

Practice Questions

334. What is a common psychological factor contributing to bureaucracy?

a. High trust

b. Paranoia about being blamed for errors

c. High levels of delegation

d. Lack of control

335. What percentage of documents retained are never used again?

a. 10%

b. 50%

c. 90%

d. 100%

336. Which organization set up a bureaucracy elimination committee to investigate unjustified activities?

a. IBM, Brazil

b. Intel

c. IBM, San Jose, California

d. None of the above

337. What is the primary tool used in the process-focused approach to identify bureaucratic steps?

a. Blue highlighter

b. Radar chart

c. Tree diagram

d. Conflict resolution techniques

338. What is the typical Return on Investment (ROI) required to justify retaining a bureaucratic activity?

Practice Questions

a. 1:1

b. 2:1

c. 3:1

d. 4:1

339. What is a significant advantage of the incident-focused approach to bureaucracy elimination?

a. It involves management only

b. It excludes employees

c. It gets the total organization involved

d. It avoids cost-benefit analysis

340. What is critical to understanding before eliminating a bureaucratic operation?

a. The cost of the operation

b. The personal opinion of employees

c. The reasons for its existence and impact on the organization

d. The number of signatures required

341. What was one of the results of Intel's attack on bureaucracy?

a. Reduced productivity

b. Increased administrative steps

c. Saved $60 million a year

d. Increased paperwork

342. What does the term "Big B" stand for in the context of bureaucracy?

a. Beneficial, beautiful, bold

b. Bad, boring, burdensome, brutal

Practice Questions

c. Best, better, bright

d. Big, bold, beautiful

343. How much managerial time is typically spent on job-related materials?

a. 10-20%

b. 30-40%

c. 40-50%

d. 60-70%

344. What is a common effect of bureaucracy on organizational efficiency?

a. Decreases paperwork

b. Speeds up processes

c. Adds resistance to progress

d. Reduces costs

345. What approach should be used to justify retaining a bureaucratic step?

a. Personal preferences

b. Data and cost-benefit analysis

c. Employee opinions

d. Number of signatures

346. What should be the focus when identifying bureaucracy in a process?

a. Increasing checks and balances

b. Reducing costs

c. Minimizing unnecessary steps

d. Adding more signatures

Practice Questions

347. What is a significant outcome of eliminating bureaucracy, as demonstrated by IBM, Brazil?

a. Creation of new procedures

b. Elimination of 50 unnecessary procedures

c. Increased use of documents

d. Increased filing cabinets

348. What technique is not typically used in conflict resolution?

a. Arbitration

b. Litigation

c. Mediation

d. Bureaucracy elimination

349. What is the first habit in Stephen Covey's model for conflict resolution?

a. Synergize

b. Think win-win

c. Be proactive

d. Begin with the end in mind

350. What is Critical to Quality (CTQ) analysis used for?

a. Identifying cost-saving measures

b. Analyzing characteristics important to the customer

c. Increasing paperwork

d. Adding bureaucratic steps

Answers

1. Answer: b. Management of organizational processes

Explanation: Lean Six Sigma (LSS) is a methodology designed to improve business processes by reducing waste and minimizing variation. The primary focus is on managing and optimizing organizational processes to achieve better quality, efficiency, and customer satisfaction. LSS combines the waste-reduction principles of Lean with the defect-reduction focus of Six Sigma, making it a powerful tool for process improvement across various industries. By focusing on organizational processes, LSS ensures that the entire system works more efficiently rather than just improving isolated parts.

2. Answer: b. To ensure a cross-functional focus for process success

Explanation: Process ownership in Lean Six Sigma is essential because it assigns responsibility for the entire process to a single individual, ensuring that the process is managed holistically rather than in silos. This cross-functional focus is critical for process success because it breaks down departmental barriers and ensures that all aspects of the process work together seamlessly. The process owner is accountable for the process's performance, which includes coordinating between different departments, resolving issues, and driving continuous improvement. This role is vital for maintaining the alignment of the process with organizational goals.

3. Answer: c. Top management, after identifying and defining the process

Explanation: In Lean Six Sigma, the selection of a process owner is a strategic decision made by top management. The process owner is typically chosen based on their knowledge, experience, and ability to influence and manage the process effectively. After the process has been identified and its boundaries defined, top management appoints a process owner who is responsible for overseeing the entire process, ensuring it meets performance objectives, and implementing improvements. This selection is crucial

Answers

because the process owner's leadership and commitment are key to the process's success and continuous improvement.

4. **Answer: c. To collectively share responsibilities related to process management**

Explanation: The Process Management Committee (PMC) in Lean Six Sigma plays a collaborative role in overseeing process management. The committee typically consists of peer-level managers from different departments who collectively share responsibilities related to managing, improving, and sustaining the process. The PMC works together to ensure that the process aligns with organizational goals, resolves any conflicts or issues that arise, and supports the process owner in achieving process objectives. By sharing these responsibilities, the PMC ensures that process management is not isolated to one individual but benefits from a collective expertise and perspective, which enhances decision-making and problem-solving.

5. **Answer: c. The focus owner**

Explanation: The Process Management Committee (PMC) is headed by the focus owner, who is typically the person with the most relevant expertise and authority over the specific process area. The focus owner leads the committee in its efforts to manage and optimize the process, ensuring that the process meets its performance goals and aligns with the organization's strategic objectives. The focus owner's leadership is critical in driving the committee's activities, coordinating efforts across different departments, and ensuring that process improvements are effectively implemented and sustained.

6. **Answer: b. They are peer-level managers**

Explanation: Members of the Process Management Committee (PMC) are typically peer-level managers from various departments involved in the process. This characteristic is important because it ensures that the committee has a broad perspective, with input from all relevant areas of the organization. Peer-level managers bring their expertise, knowledge, and

Answers

departmental insights to the committee, allowing for more informed decision-making and better coordination across the organization. By involving managers at the same level, the PMC fosters collaboration and ensures that process management decisions are made with consideration for the entire organization, not just one department.

7. Answer: c. Establishing personal performance bonuses

Explanation: The mission of the Process Management Committee (PMC) focuses on ensuring process success by steering the process toward quality objectives, supporting and committing resources, and resolving conflicts over objectives and resources. Establishing personal performance bonuses is not part of the PMC's mission. Instead, the committee is concerned with the overall performance of the process and its alignment with organizational goals. Personal performance bonuses are typically handled by other parts of the organization, such as HR or individual department management, rather than the PMC, which focuses on collective process management.

8. Answer: b. Implementing process management actions

Explanation: The Process Quality Team (PIT) is responsible for the hands-on implementation of process management and improvement actions within Lean Six Sigma. They work on the ground level to execute the strategies and plans developed by the Process Management Committee (PMC) and the process owner. The PIT is focused on applying Lean Six Sigma tools and techniques to enhance process performance, address quality issues, and ensure that the process meets its objectives. Their work is crucial for translating management decisions into actual process improvements.

9. Answer: b. The focus owner

Explanation: The Process Quality Team (PIT) is typically headed by the focus owner, who is responsible for leading the team in implementing process improvements. The focus owner is usually someone with in-depth knowledge of the process and the authority to make decisions related to its management. By heading the PIT, the focus owner ensures that the team's

Answers

efforts are aligned with the overall process objectives and that the implementation of Lean Six Sigma initiatives is effective and efficient.

10. **Answer: a. That it exists throughout the process**

Explanation: The process owner must ensure that information integrity is maintained throughout the entire process. This means that data related to the process is accurate, consistent, and reliable from start to finish. Information integrity is crucial for making informed decisions, tracking process performance, and ensuring that the process operates smoothly and efficiently. By safeguarding information integrity, the process owner can help prevent errors, reduce waste, and improve the overall quality of the process.

11. **Answer: c. To manage the entire process and ensure its success**

Explanation: The primary goal of process ownership in Lean Six Sigma is to ensure that the entire process is managed effectively and achieves its intended outcomes. The process owner is responsible for overseeing all aspects of the process, from planning and execution to monitoring and continuous improvement. By taking ownership of the process, the process owner ensures that it is aligned with organizational goals, operates efficiently, and delivers value to the customer. The success of the process is directly tied to the process owner's ability to manage it effectively.

12. **Answer: b. Via a formal announcement to all managers**

Explanation: The process owner should be introduced to their responsibilities and authority formally, typically through an announcement to all relevant managers. This formal introduction ensures that everyone in the organization is aware of the process owner's role, responsibilities, and authority in managing the process. Clear communication is essential to establish the process owner's position, gain support from other departments, and ensure that the process is managed effectively.

13. **Answer: b. being a problem fixer**

Answers

Explanation: A critical success factor for the process owner is their ability to be a "problem fixer." This means that the process owner must be proactive in identifying and resolving issues that arise within the process. By effectively addressing problems, the process owner can maintain process efficiency, reduce waste, and ensure that the process meets its performance goals. Being a problem fixer also involves continuous monitoring of the process, making adjustments as needed, and driving continuous improvement efforts.

14. Answer: d. All of the above

Explanation: Top management plays a crucial role in supporting the process owner by approving resource allocation, financing the process, and providing recognition for the process owner's efforts. These forms of support are essential for empowering the process owner to manage the process effectively. Without the backing of top management, the process owner may struggle to secure the necessary resources or authority to implement improvements, which can hinder the process's success. Top management's support is, therefore, vital for the process's overall success.

15. Answer: b. A detailed representation of the current process

Explanation: A process model should include a detailed representation of the current process, showing how it operates in its present state. This model serves as a baseline for identifying areas for improvement and for designing future-state processes. By accurately representing the current process, the model helps stakeholders understand the flow of activities, identify bottlenecks, and pinpoint opportunities for optimization. A well-documented process model is a critical tool for Lean Six Sigma projects, as it provides the foundation for analysis and improvement.

16. Answer: b. It must be clearly communicated to all concerned parties

Explanation: An important aspect of the process owner's authority is that it must be clearly communicated to all concerned parties within the organization. Clear communication ensures that everyone understands the process owner's role, the extent of their authority, and how decisions related to the process will be made. This transparency helps avoid confusion, ensures cooperation from other departments, and empowers the process owner to effectively manage the process. Without clear communication, the process owner's authority may be undermined, leading to inefficiencies and conflict.

17. Answer: a. Narrow departmental focus

Explanation: Lean Six Sigma seeks to address the issue of narrow departmental focus through process ownership. In many organizations, processes can become fragmented across departments, leading to inefficiencies and a lack of coordination. By assigning a process owner, Lean Six Sigma ensures that there is a single point of accountability for the entire process, promoting a holistic view that transcends departmental boundaries. This approach helps align the process with overall organizational goals and ensures that improvements benefit the entire organization, not just individual departments.

18. Answer: a. The process owner

Explanation:

The process owner is responsible for resolving or escalating cross-functional issues that arise during the process management. Because the process owner oversees the entire process, they are in the best position to identify issues that affect multiple departments and to take action to resolve them. If the process owner is unable to resolve an issue themselves, they have the authority to escalate it to higher management for further resolution. This responsibility is crucial for maintaining process efficiency and ensuring that cross-functional challenges do not hinder process performance.

19. Answer: a. It should be independent of operating units

Explanation: A core principle of Lean Six Sigma regarding process management is that it should be independent of operating units. This means that process management should be focused on the overall process rather

Answers

than being confined to individual departments or operating units. By managing processes independently of departmental silos, Lean Six Sigma ensures that the process is optimized for the entire organization, leading to greater efficiency and better alignment with organizational goals. This independence helps prevent conflicts of interest and promotes a more objective approach to process improvement.

20. Answer: a. Describing the process as it currently exists

Explanation: A process model should avoid describing the process solely as it currently exists if it does not also include the ideal or future state of the process. While it's important to document the current state as a baseline, Lean Six Sigma also emphasizes the need to envision and model how the process should ideally operate. By including both the current and future states, the process model can serve as a roadmap for improvement, guiding efforts to close the gap between the current and desired performance levels. Focusing only on the current state without considering the ideal state can limit the potential for significant improvements.

21. Answer: b. Defining the mission and identifying the scope

Explanation: Once ownership of a process has been established, the first step is to define the mission and identify the scope of the process. The mission statement outlines the purpose of the process and how it contributes to the organization's goals, while the scope defines the boundaries and limits of the process. This step is critical because it sets the foundation for all subsequent process management and improvement activities. By clearly defining the mission and scope, the process owner and team can focus their efforts on achieving specific objectives and avoid scope creep, which can lead to inefficiencies.

22. Answer: c. How the process helps to attain corporate goals

Explanation: The mission of a process describes how the process contributes to achieving the organization's overall goals. It explains the purpose of the process within the context of the broader organizational

Answers

strategy, providing a clear link between the process and the company's objectives. This alignment is crucial because it ensures that the process adds value to the organization and supports its long-term success. A well-defined mission statement helps guide the process owner and team in making decisions that are consistent with the organization's priorities.

23. Answer: b. Concise and to the point

Explanation: A mission statement should be concise and to the point, clearly articulating the purpose of the process without unnecessary detail or complexity. A concise mission statement is easier to communicate, understand, and remember, which helps ensure that all stakeholders are aligned with the process's objectives. It should provide a clear and focused direction for the process, helping guide decision-making and prioritization of actions.

24. Answer: c. The boundaries of the process

Explanation: The scope of a business process defines its boundaries—what the process includes and what it does not. It sets the limits on the process's activities, inputs, outputs, and interactions with other processes. Clearly defining the scope helps in focusing on specific areas of improvement, avoiding overlaps, and managing resources effectively.

25. Answer: c. Who is the process owner?

Explanation: Defining the scope of a process typically involves answering questions like "Where does the process start?", "What does the process include?", and "Where does the process end?" The question "Who is the process owner?" is related to process management, but it is not directly involved in defining the scope of the process.

26. Answer: a. Identifying the process whose mission is most clearly related to the activity in question

Explanation: When disagreements arise over the scope of a process, it is helpful to identify the process whose mission is most closely related to the

Answers

activity in question. This ensures that the activity is aligned with the correct process, helping to clarify the boundaries and responsibilities.

27. Answer: b. To avoid making assumptions

Explanation: Specifying what a process does not include is important to avoid making assumptions. It ensures that everyone involved understands the limits of the process and avoids confusion about responsibilities or activities that are outside the process's scope. This clarity helps prevent overlaps and ensures focused efforts.

28. Answer: a. When an invoice is issued, and the accounts receivable system is updated

Explanation: The accounts receivable process begins when an invoice is issued and the accounts receivable system is updated. This marks the start of tracking the customer's payment setting the stage for subsequent activities like payment collection and account reconciliation.

29. Answer: b. Collection or other settlement of customer accounts

Explanation: The accounts receivable process includes activities related to collecting or settling customer accounts. This involves ensuring that payments are received and properly recorded, and resolving any issues related to outstanding payments.

30. Answer: b. When the invoice is cleared and the accounts receivable system is updated

Explanation: The accounts receivable process ends when the invoice is cleared (i.e., the payment is received and recorded), and the accounts receivable system is updated to reflect this. This marks the completion of the process, ensuring that the customer's account is accurately maintained.

31. Answer: b. Purchasing "off the shelf" parts, equipment, or supplies from external suppliers

Answers

Explanation: The procurement process involves purchasing parts, equipment, or supplies from external suppliers. It involves sourcing, negotiating, and acquiring the necessary materials or services for the organization to operate effectively.

32. Answer: b. When the requestor submits a purchase requisition

Explanation: The procurement process begins when the requestor submits a purchase requisition. This initiates the process of identifying suppliers, obtaining quotes, and eventually purchasing the required goods or services.

33. Answer: b. Key areas of activity that must succeed for the process to achieve its goals

Explanation: Critical success factors are key areas of activity that must be successfully managed for the process to achieve its goals. These essential elements directly impact the process's success, and they require focused attention to ensure that the process delivers its intended outcomes.

34. Answer: b. The owner and the team

Explanation: The process owner and their team should write the mission and scope of a process. . This ensures that those responsible for the process have a clear understanding of its objectives, boundaries, and how it aligns with organizational goals. Collaboration in defining the mission and scope ensures that all stakeholders are on the same page and committed to the process.

35. Answer: d. Manufacturing of products

Explanation: The manufacturing of products is not included in the scope of the accounts receivable process. Accounts receivable is concerned with financial transactions related to customer payments, whereas manufacturing involves the production of goods. These are separate processes within an organization.

36. Answer: a. Staff action

Answers

Explanation: The preparation of regular reports in the accounts receivable process can be used for staff action, such as identifying overdue accounts, assessing the effectiveness of collection efforts, and making informed decisions about credit policies or customer relationships.

37. Answer: c. Notification to management of out-of-line situations

Explanation:

- **Collection of customer accounts** is part of the process but doesn't involve direct notification to management unless there's a significant issue.
- **Accurate maintenance of customer accounts** is crucial but primarily an operational task.
- **Notification to management of out-of-line situations** is essential for timely intervention and decision-making.
- **Assessing customers' creditworthiness** is part of the process but doesn't necessarily require immediate management notification.

38. Answer: c. To ensure directives are followed correctly

Explanation: Monitoring the resolution of management directives is primarily a control mechanism to verify that actions align with decisions made at a higher level. While it indirectly impacts other options, its core purpose is to ensure compliance.

39. Answer: d. Designing new products

Explanation:

- **Collection of customer accounts, preparation of regular reports,** and **monitoring resolution of management directives** are all standard functions within accounts receivable.
- **Designing new products** is a product development activity unrelated to the core functions of accounts receivable.

Answers

40. Answer: b. From manufacturing processes to business process improvement

Explanation: The 1980s marked a shift in focus from improving isolated processes (like manufacturing) to a broader perspective of enhancing overall business operations. This shift led to a more holistic approach to process improvement, considering interdependencies and the entire value chain.

41. Answer: a. Materials, machines, manpower, methods, and measurements

Explanation: The five key process inputs in Lean Six Sigma are materials, machines, manpower, methods, and measurements. These are essential for achieving customer requirements and overall organizational performance.

42. Answer: c. Value streams

Explanation: Lean accounting is aligned horizontally across the organization with value streams, simplifying the accounting process and providing real-time information.

43. Answer: b. To maintain a continuous flow of products and adapt to demand changes

Explanation: The primary idea behind the Toyota Production System is to maintain a continuous flow of products in factories, flexibly adapt to demand changes, and achieve just-in-time production.

44. Answer: b. To organize, clean, develop, and sustain a productive work environment

Explanation: The 5S methodology aims to organize, clean, develop, and sustain a productive work environment, leading to improved safety, workspace ownership, productivity, and maintenance.

45. Answer: b. Overall Equipment Effectiveness

Answers

Explanation: OEE stands for Overall Equipment Effectiveness. It is a metric used to evaluate the performance of manufacturing equipment by considering availability, performance, and quality. OEE provides insights into how effectively equipment is being used in the production process.

46. Answer: a. A type of inventory system

Explanation: A Kanban is a type of inventory system used in Lean manufacturing. It is a visual scheduling system that helps manage work and inventory levels by using cards or signals to indicate when more materials or products are needed. Kanban helps improve workflow and reduce waste.

47. Answer: a. Descriptions of the 5M's

Explanation: Value Stream Mapping typically includes descriptions of the 5M's (materials, machines, manpower, methods, and measurements) as targets for modifications in the future state.

48. Answer: c. SMED

Explanation: SMED stands for Single-Minute Exchange of Dies, a technique for reducing changeover times, thereby minimizing output and quality losses due to changeovers.

49. Answer: b. To minimize downtimes and maximize equipment usage

Explanation: The goal of Total Productive Maintenance (TPM) is to minimize downtimes and maximize equipment usage, focusing on avoiding emergency repairs and reducing unscheduled maintenance.

50. Answer: c. It needs to be understood and embraced at the highest levels of the company

Explanation: To effectively transform the organization into a lean organization, A Lean operational philosophy must be understood and embraced at the highest levels of the company, including C-level executives.

Answers

51. Answer: b. To identify and eliminate waste

Explanation: The primary objective of the LSS practitioner is to learn how to identify where wastes occur, how they occur, and what root causes led to the waste manifesting in the operation.

52. Answer: c. Customer satisfaction

Explanation: Waste is typically defined in terms of categories like overproduction, excess inventory, waiting, defects, extra processing, underutilized employees, motion, and transportation. Customer satisfaction is not a category of waste but rather a goal.

53. Answer: b. Value Added (VA) activity

Explanation: A value Added (VA) activity is any activity that the external customer is willing to pay for. It is usually comprised of the process steps required to convert raw materials into a useful product.

54. Answer: d. 95%

Explanation: Non Value Added (NVA) activities are typically extensive and can consume up to 95% of an organization's activities. These are actions that do not add value from the customer's perspective and should be minimized or eliminated to improve efficiency.

55. Answer: c. Business Value Added (BVA) activities

Explanation: Business-value-added activities are necessary for the operation of the business and to deliver products or services to the customer, even if the customer is not directly willing to pay for them. These include compliance and regulatory activities.

56. Answer: b. Question the activity

Answers

Explanation: If an activity does not add value from the customer's perspective, it should be critically evaluated. Lean Six Sigma encourages questioning such activities to determine if they can be eliminated or improved to reduce waste.

57. Answer: c. Poor-quality cost

Explanation: Poor-quality costs arise from inefficient process designs that lead to defects, rework, and waste. Addressing these costs is crucial for improving quality and reducing overall waste in a Lean Six Sigma environment.

58. Answer: b. It destroys morale

Explanation: Labeling someone's work as non Value Added (NVA) without careful consideration can negatively impact morale. It's essential to approach the topic constructively, focusing on how processes can be improved rather than criticizing the work itself.

59. Answer: c. It could destroy organizational morale

Explanation: While safety and payroll activities might not directly add value from a customer's perspective, they are essential for the operation of the business and employee well-being. Misclassifying them as non-value-added can harm morale and overlook their importance.

60. Answer: b. Waste identification

Explanation: In Lean management, the ability to see what others cannot often refers to the skill of identifying waste in processes. Recognizing inefficiencies that others might overlook is key to continuous improvement in Lean Six Sigma.

61. Answer: b. Increased defects, rework, and high scrap rates

Answers

Explanation: Weak process control leads to increased defects, rework, and high scrap rates due to deficiencies in materials, machines, manpower, methods, or measurements.

62. **Answer: d. It leads to equipment breakdowns due to poor maintenance**

Explanation: Poor maintenance can cause equipment to break down, leading to product defects. Regular and effective maintenance is crucial to ensure equipment operates correctly and produces high-quality products without defects.

63. **Answer: b. Anything that contributes to a product not meeting customer expectations**

Explanation: A defect is any flaw or issue that prevents a product from meeting customer expectations. This could be related to quality, performance, or other aspects that do not align with what the customer requires.

64. **Answer: b. Any effort that adds no value to the product or service from the customer's viewpoint**

Explanation: Processing waste refers to any activity that does not add value from the customer's perspective. This type of waste should be minimized or eliminated to improve efficiency and reduce costs in Lean Six Sigma processes.

65. **Answer: c. Extensive processing waste from several apparent causes**

Explanation: In service industries, processing waste can arise from various factors, such as unnecessary steps, poor communication, or redundant processes. Addressing these issues can significantly reduce waste and improve service delivery.

Answers

66. Answer: b. Train personnel with new instructions

Explanation: When a product or service changes, it is essential to train personnel with new instructions. This ensures that everyone understands the changes and can perform their roles effectively, minimizing errors and maintaining quality.

67. Answer: b. Making more products just in case of unforeseen issues

Explanation: Just-in-case logic refers to the practice of producing more products than necessary to account for potential issues or demands. However, this can lead to overproduction and excess inventory, which are considered waste in Lean Six Sigma.

68. Answer: c. Extra processing occurs

Explanation: When customer requirements are not clearly understood, it often leads to extra processing as attempts are made to meet the assumed needs. This results in inefficiencies and waste that could have been avoided with better communication and understanding.

69. Answer: c. Overproduction and excess inventory

Explanation:

Overprocessing to accommodate downtime can lead to overproduction and excess inventory. These are forms of waste in Lean Six Sigma, as they tie up resources without adding value from the customer's perspective.

70. Answer: b. Identifying CTQ customer requirements and transitioning them into product specifications

Explanation: In Lean Six Sigma, a typical communication cycle involves understanding the Critical to Quality (CTQ) requirements of the customer and translating these into specific product or service specifications. This ensures that the final output meets customer expectations.

Answers

71. Answer: a. Increased product cost and lead time

Explanation: Redundant approvals can slow down processes, leading to increased costs and longer lead times. In Lean Six Sigma, reducing unnecessary steps in the approval process is key to streamlining operations and improving efficiency.

72. Answer: b. It leads to information overload

Explanation: While sharing information is important, excessive information sharing can lead to overload, where key details get lost in the flood of data. This can cause delays, errors, and confusion, contributing to waste in the process.

73. Answer: c. Materials conveyance delays

Explanation: Waiting waste often occurs when there are delays in the conveyance of materials, holding up production processes. This leads to inefficiencies and increased costs, as time is wasted waiting for materials to arrive.

74. Answer: b. Raw material outages

Explanation: Raw material outages are a common root cause of waiting waste. When materials are not available as needed, it disrupts the flow of production, causing delays and inefficiencies that contribute to overall waste.

75. Answer: b. Waste of waiting

Explanation: Unbalanced workloads can delay certain parts of a process while others wait for tasks to be completed. This imbalance creates waiting waste, reducing the overall efficiency of the production process.

76. Answer: b. Waste of waiting

Explanation:

Answers

Unplanned downtime disrupts production schedules, leading to idle resources and wasted time while waiting for the equipment to be repaired. This inefficiency negatively impacts productivity and overall output.

77. Answer: b. Equipment placement based on open floor space

Explanation: If equipment is placed without considering workflow and process flow, it can lead to unnecessary movement of materials and personnel, resulting in increased waiting time. Optimal equipment placement should follow a logical sequence to minimize backtracking and maximize efficiency.

78. Answer: b. Permanent loss of time to waiting

Explanation: Long setup times can significantly delay production, resulting in a permanent loss of time due to waiting. Reducing setup times is crucial in Lean Six Sigma to maintain smooth and continuous operations.

79. Answer: a. Machines should always run to meet customer demand

Explanation: A common misconception is that machines should always run to meet demand, but running machines without regard to actual demand can lead to overproduction, excess inventory, and increased waste, contradicting Lean Six Sigma principles.

80. Answer: b. 100% first-pass quality

Explanation: The goal of every process step in Lean Six Sigma should be to achieve 100% first-pass quality, meaning that the product or service is correct and meets all specifications the first time without the need for rework or correction.

81. Answer: b. Properly connecting materials, machines, manpower, and methods

Explanation:

Answers

The ultimate objective of Lean Six Sigma is to ensure that materials, machines, manpower, and methods are all aligned and working together efficiently. This integration helps eliminate waste and improves the overall process flow.

82. Answer: c. Inconsistent work methods

Explanation: Inconsistent work methods can lead to unnecessary motion, as employees may have to move around more to complete their tasks. Standardizing work methods helps reduce motion waste and increases efficiency.

83. Answer: c. By causing manual document transfers and information exchange delays

Explanation: Poor information management can lead to delays in the transfer of documents and information, which in turn can create bottlenecks and waste. Efficient information flow is critical to maintaining smooth operations.

84. Answer: b. Creating standard operating procedures or visual work instructions

Explanation: Establishing Standard Operating Procedures (SOPs) or visual work instructions helps to standardize tasks, reducing variation and the waste that comes from inconsistent work methods. This ensures everyone follows the same best practices.

85. Answer: b. Significant motion, transportation, and waiting wastes

Explanation: Poor facility or cell layout can result in significant waste due to increased motion, transportation, and waiting times. A well-designed layout minimizes these wastes by ensuring that equipment and processes are logically and efficiently arranged.

86. Answer: b. Manual transportation of documents

Explanation:

Answers

In administrative areas, manual document transportation is a common source of motion waste. Better document management systems and process digitization can reduce this unnecessary movement.

87. Answer: c. Poor workplace organization and housekeeping

Explanation: Poor workplace organization and housekeeping can lead to motion waste, as employees may have to search for tools or materials. A well-organized workspace reduces unnecessary movement and increases efficiency.

88. Answer: b. By increasing the need for hand delivery of materials

Explanation: When processes are not optimized, employees may need to manually handle or deliver materials, leading to increased motion waste. Automation and better process design can reduce the need for such interactions.

89. Answer: c. Inconsistent learning and practices

Explanation: Tribal knowledge refers to unwritten, informal knowledge held by a few individuals.

Not everyone has access to the same information, which can lead to inconsistencies in task performance and potential waste.

90. Answer: b. The root cause of product or service quality issues

Explanation: Poorly documented work methods can be the root cause of quality issues, as employees may not follow consistent procedures. Proper documentation helps ensure that everyone follows the same process, leading to higher quality and reduced waste.

91. Answer: a. Increased lead time

Explanation: Poor facility layout often results in increased lead times due to inefficient material flow, unnecessary transportation, and delays. A well-designed layout minimizes these issues, leading to faster and more efficient

Answers

production.

92. Answer: b. To identify where and when motion waste occurs

Explanation: The objective of learning to see motion waste is to recognize where and when unnecessary movements occur in the process. By identifying these wastes, steps can be taken to reduce or eliminate them, improving efficiency.

93. Answer: c. Both people and equipment

Explanation: Transportation waste involves the unnecessary movement of both people and equipment. It can occur when processes are not optimally designed, leading to inefficient resource use.

94. Answer: b. Poor purchasing practices

Explanation: Poor purchasing practices, such as ordering large batches or not considering the layout, can lead to excessive transportation waste. Efficient purchasing and inventory management are crucial to minimizing unnecessary movement.

95. Answer: b. It leads to transportation waste and other types of waste

Explanation: Poor purchasing practices can result in excess inventory, requiring more movement to store and retrieve items, thus increasing transportation waste. This can also contribute to other types of waste, such as overproduction and excess inventory.

96. Answer: c. Productivity and profitability

Explanation: An inadequate facility layout directly impacts productivity and profitability by creating inefficiencies in material flow, increasing transportation waste, and causing delays. A well-designed layout is essential for maximizing efficiency and profitability.

97. Answer: c. Small storage areas

Answers

Explanation: Small storage areas themselves do not necessarily cause transportation waste. Instead, issues like poor purchasing practices, large batch sizes, and inadequate facility layout are more likely to contribute to transportation waste.

98. Answer: b. To understand process flow deeply

Explanation: The primary goal of Lean Six Sigma practitioners is to deeply understand process flows to identify and eliminate waste, optimize efficiency, and improve quality. This comprehensive understanding allows for targeted improvements and sustainable gains.

99. Answer: b. Visualizing processes that should be next to each other

Explanation: Mapping product flows helps visualize how processes are connected and which ones should be positioned close to each other to reduce transportation waste and improve efficiency. It's a key step in optimizing facility layout and process design.

100. Answer: b. Low pay and high turnover strategy

Explanation: Strategies like low pay and high turnover can waste underutilized employees by failing to fully leverage their skills and potential. Effective employee utilization involves proper training, development, and engagement strategies.

101. Answer: b. Low pay and high turnover rate

Explanation: Traditional organizations often offer lower salaries compared to more modern firms. This can lead to higher turnover rates as employees leave for better-paying opportunities. Low compensation might also impact employee morale and retention.

102. Answer: b. Waste of waiting

Explanation:

Answers

A well-designed facility layout minimizes unnecessary delays by optimizing workflows and reducing waiting times. Proper placement of equipment and workstations can streamline processes and enhance efficiency.

103. Answer: b. It can be extremely damaging

Explanation: Behavior waste, such as poor communication and ineffective work habits, can significantly negatively impact productivity and morale. It can lead to inefficiencies, lower-quality output, and a toxic work environment.

104. Answer: c. Underutilized employees waste

Explanation: This type of waste occurs when employees' skills and talents are not fully leveraged. It can result from poor job design, lack of proper training, or insufficient opportunities for employees to contribute effectively.

105. Answer: d. Not getting the best candidate for the position

Explanation: Poor hiring practices can lead to hiring individuals who are not the best fit for the job. This can result in lower productivity, increased turnover, and higher recruitment costs as the organization struggles to find suitable replacements.

106. Answer: b. Higher-performing companies tend to invest more in training

Explanation: Companies that perform well often recognize the value of investing in employee training. This investment helps improve skills, enhance productivity, and ultimately contributes to better overall company performance.

107. Answer: b. When and where motion waste occurs

Explanation: The waste of motion checklist pinpoints unnecessary movements and process inefficiencies. By identifying where and when these

Answers

wastes occur, organizations can streamline operations and reduce wasteful activities.

108. **Answer: c. Poor working conditions**

Explanation: Low pay combined with high turnover often reflects poor working conditions. Employees are less likely to stay in environments where compensation is inadequate and working conditions are unsatisfactory, leading to frequent staff changes.

109. **Answer: b. The path across the organization that adds value for the customer**

Explanation: The value stream encompasses all the activities and processes that contribute to delivering value to the customer. It includes every step from production to delivery, focusing on optimizing each step to enhance customer satisfaction.

110. **Answer: b. To focus on external customer response**

Explanation: Value stream management aims to optimize the flow of value to the customer by streamlining processes and eliminating waste. The focus is on improving responsiveness and meeting customer needs more effectively.

111. **Answer: c. Flow chart**

Explanation: A flowchart is commonly used to identify Critical to Quality (CTQ) parameters by visually mapping out processes and highlighting areas that impact product or service quality. This helps in focusing on key factors that affect overall quality.

112. **Answer: b. Reduce the time to move an item through a process**

Explanation:

Answers

Cycle time analysis and reduction aim to shorten the duration it takes to complete a process. Reducing cycle time enhances efficiency, decreases costs, and improves customer satisfaction by speeding up delivery.

113. Answer: b. Supplier certification

Explanation: Supplier certification is a recognized best practice that ensures suppliers meet quality standards and contribute to the overall quality of the final product. It helps in maintaining consistency and reliability in the supply chain.

114. Answer: c. Increasing interruptions

Explanation: Increasing interruptions actually lengthens cycle time rather than reducing it. Effective cycle time reduction involves optimizing processes, eliminating bottlenecks, and improving workflow efficiency.

115. Answer: b. Increased storage costs

Explanation: Long cycle times can lead to higher storage costs as products remain in inventory longer. This can also affect cash flow and overall efficiency, impacting the business's ability to respond quickly to market demands.

116. Answer: b. Reduced to 8 steps

Explanation: Intel's efforts to eliminate bureaucracy significantly streamlined the process, reducing the number of administrative steps required to purchase a simple item like a ballpoint pen from a much larger number to just 8 steps.

117. Answer: b. Understand its purpose and impact

Explanation: Before removing a bureaucratic activity, it is crucial to understand its purpose and potential impact. This ensures that valuable functions are not inadvertently eliminated and helps maintain necessary controls and processes.

Answers

118. **Answer: b. Increased delays**

Explanation: Bureaucracy often leads to increased delays due to excessive procedures, approvals, and red tape. This can slow down decision-making processes and affect overall organizational efficiency.

119. **Answer: d. 90%**

Explanation: A significant portion of clerical work, around 90%, is typically dedicated to activities like checking, filing, and retrieving information. This highlights the need for more efficient information management systems.

120. **Answer: b. Financially justifying every approval signature**

Explanation: A key objective in tackling bureaucracy is to ensure that every approval and signature is financially justified. This helps streamline processes, reduce unnecessary approvals, and improve overall efficiency.

121. **Answer: b. Reducing the time products spend in storage**

Explanation: Continuous flow aims to create a smooth, uninterrupted flow of products through the production process, minimizing inventory build-up and reducing lead times.

122. **Answer: b. Replenishes materials based on customer demand**

Explanation: Pull systems ensure that production and material replenishment are driven by actual customer demand, reducing overproduction.

123. **Answer: b. Locating materials at the point of value-adding activities**

Explanation: Point-of-use storage places materials exactly where they are needed for value-adding activities, reducing transportation waste.

124. **Answer: b. Building quality into processes as they are completed**

Answers

Explanation: Quality at source aims to ensure that quality is built into each step of the process rather than inspecting for quality afterward.

125. Answer: c. The demand rate of the external customer

Explanation: Takt time represents the rate at which products need to be produced to meet customer demand. It is calculated by dividing available production time by customer demand, helping to balance production rates with market needs.

126. Answer: b. Lean management concepts

Explanation: Successful Lean programs rely on the implementation of Lean management concepts, which focus on eliminating waste, improving processes, and enhancing value for the customer. These principles are essential for achieving Lean objectives.

127. Answer: b. Causes of transportation waste

Explanation: The waste of transportation checklist is used to identify sources of waste related to the movement of materials. By pinpointing causes, organizations can reduce unnecessary transportation and streamline logistics.

128. Answer: b. Waste

Explanation: In Lean terminology, "muda" refers to any activity or process that does not add value and is considered waste. Identifying and eliminating muda is crucial for improving efficiency and reducing unnecessary costs.

129. Answer: b. Human interactions

Explanation: Ineffective human interactions, such as poor communication or unproductive work habits primarily cause behavior waste. These inefficiencies can disrupt workflows and negatively impact overall performance.

130. Answer: c. Restricted process improvement

Answers

Explanation: Waste generated by employees, such as inefficient work practices or errors, can hinder process improvement efforts. Addressing these issues is essential for enhancing overall productivity and achieving better results.

131 Answer: a. Quantitative and Qualitative

Explanation: Visual techniques involve directly observing processes to identify waste, while analytical techniques use data and metrics to pinpoint inefficiencies. Both methods are important for effective waste identification and management.

132. Answer: b. Qualitative techniques

Explanation: The Lean aspect of Lean Six Sigma (LSS) emphasizes qualitative techniques, such as process mapping and value stream analysis, to identify and eliminate waste. These techniques are crucial for improving process efficiency and effectiveness.

133. Answer: c. Point of Use Storage

Explanation: Point of Use Storage (POUS) involves keeping materials and tools at the location where they are needed for production. This reduces transportation time and increases efficiency by ensuring resources are readily accessible.

134. Answer: d. Managing all aspects of value creation for the customer

Explanation: Value stream management focuses on overseeing and optimizing every aspect of the value creation process to ensure that value is delivered to the customer efficiently. This involves improving processes and eliminating waste throughout the value stream.

135. Answer: b. Waiting

Answers

Explanation: Continuous flow aims to eliminate waiting waste by ensuring that work progresses smoothly through each stage of production. This approach helps to minimize delays and improve overall process efficiency.

136. **Answer: b. Information management, documentation management, or activity management**

Explanation: In service industries, the value stream often involves managing information and activities rather than physical materials.

137. **Answer: b. Multiple stakeholders with different views of value**

Explanation: Government agencies often face challenges in identifying the value stream due to the presence of multiple stakeholders who may have varying perspectives on what constitutes value. This can complicate efforts to streamline processes and improve efficiency.

138. **Answer: c. Mistake proofing**

Explanation: Mistake proofing, also known as poka-yoke, is a tool used to achieve quality at the source by designing processes that prevent errors and defects from occurring. This approach helps ensure that quality issues are addressed during production.

139. **Answer: a. Change for the better**

Explanation: "Kaizen" is a Japanese term meaning "change for the better." It refers to the continuous improvement philosophy that involves making incremental changes to enhance processes, efficiency, and overall performance.

140. **Answer: a. Materials, Machines, Manpower, Methods, and Measurements**

Explanation: The 5M's in Lean Six Sigma are Materials, Machines, Manpower, Methods, and Measurements. These elements represent key factors that can impact process performance and quality, and addressing them is essential for effective process improvement.

Copyright © 2024 VERSAtile Reads. All rights reserved.

Answers

141. Answer: b. Fishbone Diagram

Explanation: The Fishbone Diagram (also known as an Ishikawa or cause-and-effect diagram) is used to systematically identify potential causes of a problem. It helps teams visualize relationships between various potential causes and the overall effect, making it an ideal tool for root cause analysis.

142. Answer: a. Just-in-Time

Explanation: Just-in-Time (JIT) is a concept that ensures resources are only utilized in response to actual customer demand. This approach helps minimize excess inventory and reduces waste by aligning production with demand.

143. Answer: b. Quality at the source

Explanation: Quality at the source is integral to new or revised processes in Lean because it emphasizes addressing quality issues during production rather than after the fact. This helps ensure higher quality outputs and reduces rework.

144. Answer: c. Minimizing inventory carrying costs

Explanation: The ultimate goal of Just-in-Time (JIT) is to minimize inventory carrying costs by producing and delivering items only as needed. This approach helps reduce excess inventory and associated holding costs.

145. Answer: b. Waiting

Explanation: Poor quality of information often leads to waiting waste, as delays occur while waiting for accurate or complete information. This can slow down processes and impact overall efficiency.

146. Answer: b. VA and NVA waste activities

Answers

Explanation: The value stream in an organization includes both Value Added (VA) and Non Value Added (NVA) activities. Identifying and optimizing these activities is essential for improving process efficiency and enhancing value delivery.

147. Answer: b. Through value stream mapping

Explanation: Value stream mapping is used to visualize the value stream in Lean Six Sigma. It provides a graphical representation of processes and helps identify areas for improvement by mapping out both value-adding and waste activities.

148. Answer: c. Effective waste identification and Lean concept/tool selection

Explanation: A successful waste elimination plan requires effective identification of waste and the appropriate selection of Lean concepts and tools. This ensures that waste is accurately addressed and process improvements are effectively implemented.

149. Answer: b. Inventory turns

Explanation: Just-in-Time (JIT) is a lean manufacturing methodology aimed at reducing inventory and increasing efficiency. A key business measure related to JIT is inventory turns, which measures how often inventory is sold or used during a specific period. This metric is crucial because JIT aims to minimize inventory levels, thereby reducing carrying costs and waste. High inventory turns indicate that the company is efficiently managing its inventory, keeping it low and only replenishing it as needed, which aligns perfectly with the principles of JIT.

150. Answer: c. Producing quality at each VA step

Explanation: Quality at the Source is a Lean principle where every worker or operator in the production process is responsible for ensuring that the quality of the product meets standards at each step. Instead of relying on final inspections to catch defects, this approach emphasizes building quality

Answers

into the product at each **value-adding step.** This not only helps in reducing defects and rework but also ensures that problems are identified and corrected immediately, minimizing waste and improving overall process efficiency.

151. Answer: b. Identifying waste through POUS

Explanation: Qualitative waste identification involves subjective assessments, such as observing waste at the Point of Use Storage (POUS). This contrasts with quantitative methods, which involve statistical measurements. Identifying waste through POUS focuses on visual and intuitive recognition of inefficiencies in the work environment.

152. Answer: b. Lead time

Explanation: Continuous flow refers to the smooth and uninterrupted movement of products or information through the process. By maintaining a continuous flow, organizations can reduce lead time—the time it takes from the start to the completion of a process. This reduction in lead time can improve overall efficiency and customer satisfaction.

153. Answer: c. Financial auditing

Explanation: Value stream management focuses on the flow of materials and information required to bring a product or service to the customer. It includes components like vendor relationships, operational philosophy, and performance measurement. Financial auditing, however, is a separate function that deals with financial records and is not a direct component of value stream management.

154. Answer: b. Navy

Explanation: The U.S. Navy has successfully applied value stream management principles to improve efficiency in various processes. This application has allowed the Navy to streamline operations, reduce waste, and enhance value delivery in its logistical and operational systems.

Answers

155. Answer: c. Design of Experiments (DOE)

Explanation: DOE is a statistical tool used to determine the relationship between factors affecting a process and the output of that process. It helps identify the most critical variables (inputs) and their effects on process performance.

156. Answer: c. Understanding all value stream components

Explanation: A central activity for a Lean practitioner is to understand all components of the value stream. This understanding enables them to identify and eliminate waste, improve processes, and ensure that every step in the process adds value to the customer.

157. Answer: b. All VA steps

Explanation: The concept of flow in Lean aims to link all Value Added (VA) steps seamlessly to create a smooth and continuous process. The goal is to ensure that each step in the process moves efficiently without delays or bottlenecks, enhancing overall productivity.

158. Answer: a. Key Process Input Variables

Explanation: KPIVs (Key Process Input Variables) are the critical factors that affect the outcome of a process. In Lean Six Sigma, these variables are identified, controlled, and optimized to improve process performance and achieve desired results.

159. Answer: b. To visualize the entire value stream

Explanation: The primary purpose of value stream mapping is to visualize the entire value stream from the start to the end of the process. This tool helps organizations identify waste, inefficiencies, and opportunities for improvement, leading to a more streamlined and value-driven process.

160. Answer: c. Continuous flow

Answers

Explanation: Continuous flow is often described as the "Holy Grail" in Lean manufacturing or service delivery. It refers to the ideal state where products or services move smoothly through each step of the process without delays, interruptions, or excessive inventory, leading to maximum efficiency and customer satisfaction.

161. Answer: b. More effective use of resources

Explanation: The primary target of organizational process improvement programs, such as Lean and Six Sigma, is to make more effective use of resources. This includes reducing waste, improving efficiency, and optimizing processes to deliver better value to customers.

162. Answer: b. Statistical Process Control (SPC)

Explanation: SPC is a method used to monitor and control a process through the use of statistical tools, allowing organizations to maintain process consistency and detect variations before they become problematic.

163. Answer: b. Organize housekeeping activities and standardize materials, machinery, manpower, and methodologies

Explanation: The 5S methodology aims to organize and standardize the workplace to improve efficiency, safety, and productivity. It involves organizing housekeeping activities and standardizing materials, machinery, manpower, and methodologies to create a more effective work environment.

164. Answer: a. Sort

Explanation: The "Sort" phase of 5S involves eliminating anything that is not needed in the work area. This step helps to clear out clutter, make the workspace more organized, and ensure that only necessary items are available, leading to increased efficiency.

165. Answer: b. Ensure the entire area is completely clean

Answers

Explanation: The "Shine" phase of 5S focuses on thoroughly cleaning the work area. This step ensures that the workplace is clean, orderly, and well-maintained, which not only improves safety and efficiency but also boosts morale and pride in the workplace.

166. Answer: a. Developing the discipline to maintain the 5S program

Explanation: The "Sustain" phase of 5S is about developing the discipline to maintain the improvements achieved in the previous steps. It involves regular checks, continuous training, and reinforcement of the standards set to ensure the workplace remains organized and efficient.

167. Answer: b. Having too many internally focused measures

Explanation: A common mistake organizations make when implementing Key Process Output Variables (KPOVs) is focusing too much on internally focused measures. While internal measures are important, they should be balanced with external measures (like customer satisfaction) to ensure that the process improvements align with overall business goals.

168. Answer: c. Scatter Plots

Explanation: Scatter plots visually represent the relationship between two variables, allowing practitioners to identify correlations or trends that may indicate a relationship during the Analyze phase of DMAIC.

169. Answer: d. Employee satisfaction

Explanation: The three direct measurements of Overall Equipment Effectiveness (OEE) are equipment availability, equipment performance, and product quality. While employee satisfaction is important, it is not a direct component of OEE.

170. Answer: b. Minimize or eliminate mistakes

Explanation: The primary purpose of mistake-proofing (also known as poka-yoke) is to minimize or eliminate mistakes in processes. This Lean tool

Answers

is designed to prevent errors from occurring, thereby improving quality and reducing the need for rework.

171. Answer: a. PDCA cycle

Explanation: The PDCA (Plan-Do-Check-Act) cycle is typically used in mistake-proofing. This iterative process helps in planning the mistake-proofing measures, implementing them, checking their effectiveness, and then acting to make necessary adjustments.

172. Answer: a. Organize VA activities into the most effective and least resource-consuming series of activities

Explanation: The primary goal of cellular manufacturing is to organize value-adding (VA) activities into the most effective and least resource-consuming series of activities. This approach helps to streamline production, reduce waste, and increase efficiency by grouping machines and processes into cells.

173. Answer: a. Chart the current work sequence

Explanation: The first step in creating manufacturing cells is to chart the current work sequence. This involves mapping out the existing process flow to understand how work currently moves through the system. This information is critical for designing efficient manufacturing cells.

174. Answer: d. Standardize

Explanation: The "Standardize" phase of 5S is often the most challenging for organizations to maintain. This phase involves setting and maintaining high standards for workplace organization, which requires consistent effort and discipline over time to ensure that improvements are sustained.

175. Answer: c. Kanban

Explanation: Kanban is a Lean tool that uses visual signals (such as cards or boards) to make the requirement for action visible to employees. It helps

Answers

manage workflow by indicating when to start or stop production based on demand, thereby preventing overproduction and reducing waste.

176. Answer: a. Signal

Explanation: In Japanese, "Kanban" literally means "card" or "signboard." In the context of Lean, Kanban refers to the visual cards or signals used to control the flow of work and inventory in a production process.

177. Answer: b. Produce only what the customer requested

Explanation: The primary benefit of using Kanban is that it helps produce only what the customer requests. This approach aligns production closely with actual customer demand, reducing excess inventory, minimizing waste, and improving efficiency.

178. Answer: c. Construct a current state map

Explanation: The first step in Value Stream Mapping (VSM) is to construct a current state map. This map provides a detailed view of the existing process, including all the steps involved in delivering a product or service. Understanding the current state is essential before making improvements.

179. Answer: a. It defines and outlines how you want your organization to perform in the future

Explanation: The future state map in VSM is important because it defines and outlines how you want your organization to perform in the future. This map serves as a blueprint for making improvements, guiding the transformation from the current state to the desired future state.

180. Answer: d. Supervise

Explanation: The 5S program includes the phases: Sort, Set-in-order, Shine, Standardize, and Sustain. "Supervise" is not one of the phases in the 5S methodology.

Answers

181. Answer: a. Simplify material flow

Explanation: The primary purpose of creating a cell in cellular manufacturing is to simplify material flow. By grouping processes and machines into cells, material and information can move more smoothly and efficiently through the production process, reducing waste and increasing productivity.

182. Answer: a. Cleaning schedules

Explanation: Cleaning schedules are a common tool for sustaining the 5S program. Regular cleaning and maintenance help to maintain the improvements made during the initial phases of 5S, ensuring that the workplace remains organized, safe, and efficient.

183. Answer: b. Identify items that are wanted but not needed

Explanation: The purpose of a red tag in the 'Sort' phase of 5S is to identify items that are wanted but not needed in the work area. These items are typically moved to a holding area for further evaluation, and if they are not necessary, they are removed from the workspace.

184. Answer: b. Improve productivity

Explanation: The primary focus of Lean tools is to improve productivity by eliminating waste, streamlining processes, and enhancing efficiency. These tools are designed to help organizations deliver value to customers more effectively and with fewer resources.

185. Answer: d. Increase marketing budget

Explanation: The key steps in the successful design and implementation of a manufacturing cell include grouping products, measuring demand, and combining work and balancing processes. Increasing the marketing budget is not related to the design and implementation of manufacturing cells.

Answers

186. Answer: a. To set items in order of use

Explanation: The main objective of the 'Set-in-order' phase in 5S is to arrange items in the order of use, making them easily accessible and reducing the time spent searching for tools and materials. This organization helps to improve efficiency and workflow.

187. Answer: a. Value-Added

Explanation: In the context of Lean Six Sigma, VA stands for "Value-Added." This term refers to any activity that adds value to the product or service from the customer's perspective. Lean focuses on maximizing VA activities while minimizing or eliminating non-value-added activities.

188. Answer: b. Create a safe, neat, orderly workplace

Explanation: One key benefit of implementing an effective 5S program is creating a safe, neat, and orderly workplace. By organizing the work environment, 5S helps to improve safety, reduce waste, and increase efficiency, leading to a more productive and pleasant workspace.

189. Answer: a. Clean and sweep the entire area

Explanation: A critical component of the 'Shine' phase in 5S is to clean and sweep the entire area. This step ensures that the workplace is free of dirt, debris, and clutter, which helps maintain a high level of cleanliness and organization.

190. Answer: a. To maintain a consistent application of 5S activities

Explanation: It is important to use standardized tools in the 'Standardize' phase of 5S to ensure a consistent application of 5S activities across the organization. Standardization helps to embed the 5S practices into the daily routine, making it easier to sustain the improvements over time.

191. Answer: b. Understanding the nature of the measurement system

Answers

Explanation: Understanding the nature of the measurement system is critical for the success of a Lean Six Sigma (LSS) project. Accurate and reliable measurements are essential for identifying areas for improvement, tracking progress, and ensuring that the process improvements are effective.

192. Answer: c. Department measures

Explanation: Financial measures should be considered when formulating an LSS project, as they provide insight into the economic impact of the process improvements. These measures help organizations understand the cost-benefit ratio and ensure that the LSS project delivers tangible financial results.

193. Answer: c. Technological innovation measures

Explanation: Technological innovation measures are not typically a factor that influences resistance to change in an LSS project. Individual employee performance measures, customer-related performance measures, and regulatory agency measures more commonly influence resistance to change.

194. Answer: b. Challenging current beliefs and practices

Explanation: A fundamental characteristic of operating in a Lean Six Sigma (LSS) environment is challenging current beliefs and practices. This approach encourages continuous improvement and innovation by questioning the status quo and seeking better ways to achieve process efficiency and quality.

195. Answer: b. Letting go of old beliefs

Explanation: The first step in rewriting beliefs to transition to an LSS environment is letting go of old beliefs. This involves recognizing that current practices may not be the most effective and being open to adopting new ways of thinking and working.

196. Answer: c. Opening up the mind to new ways of thinking

Answers

Explanation: The second phase in successfully transitioning to a new set of beliefs and behaviors in an LSS environment is opening up the mind to new ways of thinking. This phase is crucial for embracing the changes required to implement LSS principles effectively.

197. **Answer: b. The activities they conduct and whether they create value for the customer**

Explanation: In an LSS environment, employees should question their daily activities and whether they create value for the customer. This practice ensures that all actions are aligned with the goal of delivering value and eliminating waste.

198. **Answer: b. Hypothesis Testing**

Explanation: Hypothesis testing is a statistical method used to determine if there is enough evidence to support a specific claim about a process. It is used in Six Sigma to compare before-and-after scenarios to confirm whether process improvements are significant and not due to random variation.

199. **Answer: b. Radical changes**

Explanation: Kaikaku refers to radical changes or large-scale improvements that significantly impact the organization. Unlike Kaizen, which focuses on gradual, continuous improvement, Kaikaku involves making substantial, transformative changes to processes or systems.

200. **Answer: b. Developing a learning environment**

Explanation: The essence of considering new possibilities in an LSS environment is developing a learning environment. This involves fostering a culture of continuous learning and improvement, where employees are encouraged to explore new ideas, experiment with different approaches, and share knowledge.

201. **Answer: b. Continued practice of leaving old beliefs behind and considering new possibilities**

Answers

Explanation: Lean Six Sigma (LSS) environments thrive on continuous improvement, which requires challenging existing beliefs and being open to new approaches. This mindset is essential for fostering innovation and ensuring that processes are continually optimized for efficiency and quality.

202. Answer: d. Going to Gemba

Explanation: The first step in Kaizen process troubleshooting is to "Go to Gemba," which means visiting the actual place where the work is done. This allows teams to observe processes in real-time, gather relevant information, and understand the issues directly from the source.

203. Answer: b. Implement the plan

Explanation: The "Do" phase of the PDCA (Plan-Do-Check-Act) cycle involves implementing the plan that was developed during the "Plan" phase. This step is critical for testing the proposed changes in a controlled manner.

204. Answer: a. Kusai

Explanation: The four K's of Kaizen typically refer to "Kiken" (danger), "Kitsui" (difficulty), "Kitanai" (uncleanliness), and "Kakushin" (innovation). "Kusai," which means "smelly" in Japanese, is not part of this framework.

205. Answer: a. Maintenance and improvement

Explanation: In a Lean organization, management's role is to maintain existing processes while continuously seeking opportunities for improvement. This dual focus ensures that operations remain efficient while evolving to meet new challenges and opportunities.

206. Answer: b. Conduct Gembutsu

Explanation: "Conduct Gembutsu" is the step in which all relevant information is gathered and assessed. This step is crucial for understanding

Answers

the problem fully and ensuring that any actions taken are based on accurate data and observations.

207. Answer: c. Standardize the use of the new procedure

Explanation: To prevent problems from recurring, it's essential to standardize the new procedures that were developed as a result of the troubleshooting process. This ensures that the improved processes are consistently applied across the organization.

208. Answer: b. Cross-functional collaboration for process improvement

Explanation: Kaizen teams are typically cross-functional, bringing together diverse perspectives and expertise. This collaboration enhances the effectiveness of process improvement initiatives by leveraging a broad range of insights and skills.

209. Answer: a. Select target area

Explanation: Preparing for a Kaizen event begins with selecting the target area where improvements are most needed. This focus helps ensure that the event addresses critical issues and yields significant benefits.

210. Answer: b. Mentor team members and provide objective insights

Explanation: An external consultant in a Kaizen event acts as a mentor, offering guidance and objective insights that can help the team see beyond internal biases and develop more effective solutions.

211. Answer: b. The "we can't" syndrome

Explanation: The "we can't" syndrome is a major obstacle in Kaizen, as it reflects a mindset resistant to change. Overcoming this barrier is crucial for enabling continuous improvement and fostering a culture of innovation.

212. Answer: b. Implementing temporary measures only

Answers

Explanation: A common mistake is relying solely on temporary measures, which may not address the root cause of the problem. To ensure lasting improvements, it's important to follow through with permanent solutions and process standardization.

213. Answer: b. Process improvement

Explanation: Kaizen teams should focus on process improvement, continuously seeking ways to enhance efficiency, quality, and overall performance in line with Lean principles.

214. Answer: b. Development of new processes

Explanation: Lean management in an LSS environment centers on the development and continuous improvement of processes, ensuring they are efficient, effective, and aligned with organizational goals.

215. Answer: a. Participate and share ideas

Explanation: Employees play a crucial role in Kaizen by actively participating and sharing ideas for improvement. Their involvement is key to identifying issues and generating solutions that enhance process efficiency and effectiveness.

216. Answer: c. Determine whether implementation has brought planned improvement

Explanation: In the "Check" phase of the PDCA cycle, the focus is on evaluating whether the changes implemented during the "Do" phase have led to the desired improvements. This assessment is critical for deciding whether to standardize the changes or make further adjustments.

217. Answer: d. Standardize the new procedures

Explanation: The "Act" phase involves standardizing the new procedures that have been validated during the "Check" phase. This ensures that the

Answers

improvements become part of the regular processes and are consistently applied.

218. Answer: c. Standardize the new procedures

Explanation: Standardizing new procedures is essential in Kaizen for preventing the recurrence of problems. It ensures that successful changes are consistently implemented across the organization, reducing the likelihood of the same issues arising again.

219. Answer: b. Revise preparation and focus

Explanation: If a Kaizen event doesn't produce the expected results, it's important to revisit the preparation and focus areas. This review can help identify where adjustments are needed to improve the effectiveness of future events.

220. Answer: b. Enhanced idea generation and creativity

Explanation: Cross-functional teams bring together diverse perspectives, enhancing idea generation and creativity. This diversity is a major advantage in Kaizen, as it fosters innovative solutions and comprehensive improvements.

221. Answer: c. Beliefs determine how employees act and respond.

Explanation: In Lean Six Sigma, the concept that "beliefs drive behavior" emphasizes that employees' and management's mindsets and beliefs directly influence their actions and reactions.

222. Answer: b. Challenge the response by exploring what could be done if the change were possible.

Explanation: The response, "I know we can't do this because, but if we could, how would we?" encourages creative problem-solving and overcomes resistance to change.

Answers

223. Answer: b. Repeat the Kaizen process.

Explanation: A Kaizen event is an iterative process. If initial attempts don't yield the desired results, it's essential to analyze what went wrong, learn from the experience, and try again with adjustments. Abandoning Kaizen or blaming employees is counterproductive.

224. Answer: b. Radical transformation or innovation.

Explanation: Kaikaku is the Japanese term for radical, breakthrough improvement. It involves significant changes to processes, systems, or technologies to achieve dramatic results, unlike Kaizen, which focuses on small, incremental improvements.

225. Answer: b. Focuses on results rather than processes.

Explanation: Kaizen is fundamentally about improving processes. While results are important, the emphasis is on identifying and eliminating waste within the process to achieve continuous improvement.

226. Answer: b. Lean is just a set of tools.

Explanation: The misconception is that Lean is merely a set of tools, whereas true Lean transformation requires a change in beliefs and mindset.

227. Answer: c. Consideration of customer demand.

Explanation: A true Lean facility layout is designed with the flow of materials and customer demand in mind. This approach ensures that the layout supports efficient operations and meets customer needs effectively.

228. Answer: b. Customer demand.

Explanation: The primary focus when designing a new facility layout in a Lean environment should be customer demand. The layout should facilitate

Answers

the efficient flow of materials and processes that directly respond to customer needs.

229. **Answer: b. To visualize and test the layout before implementation.**

Explanation: A "walk-through" Lean layout is used to visualize and test the design before full implementation. This helps identify potential issues and allows for adjustments to be made to optimize the layout for efficiency and effectiveness.

230. **Answer: b. Radical transformation**

Explanation: Kakushin refers to radical transformation, similar to Kaikaku. It involves significant, often disruptive, changes that aim to fundamentally improve processes or systems.

231. **Answer: b. Revenue growth.**

Explanation: As highlighted in Lean principles, corporations' new strategic mantra is revenue growth rather than cost-cutting. This shift emphasizes the importance of creating value and driving long-term success.

232. **Answer: c. Six.**

Explanation: The 20-20 innovation process consists of six essentials, each focusing on different aspects of innovation and strategic planning.

233. **Answer: a. Generate the mindset.**

Explanation: This essential involves creating a strategy for various alternative points of view and developing the right attitudes for success.

234. **Answer: b. Acquiring strategic knowledge.**

Explanation: In the "Know the territory" stage, the primary skill needed is acquiring strategic knowledge. This involves understanding the

Answers

environment, market, and potential challenges that could impact the innovation process.

235. Answer: b. Cultivating quality communications and interaction.

Explanation: "Build the relationships" focuses on cultivating effective communication and interactions. Strong relationships are essential for collaboration, trust, and successful implementation of innovation strategies.

236. Answer: c. Choosing projects and defining strategies.

Explanation: The "Manage the journeys" stage is about selecting the right projects and defining the strategies needed to achieve innovation goals. It's a critical phase for ensuring that resources are effectively aligned with strategic objectives.

237. Answer: c. Designing end-to-end solutions.

Explanation: The "Create the solutions" stage involves designing comprehensive, end-to-end solutions that address the challenges identified earlier in the process. This stage is about turning ideas into actionable plans.

238. Answer: a. Discoverer

Explanation: The "Discoverer" personality is linked to the "Generate the mindset" essential, as this role involves exploring new ideas, identifying opportunities, and challenging existing paradigms to foster innovation.

239. Answer: a. Engineer

Explanation: An engineer, often involved in problem-solving and innovation, is likely to take on the "Discoverer" role in the 20-20 innovation process. This role focuses on exploring new possibilities and generating ideas.

240. Answer: b. Implementing effective solutions.

Answers

Explanation: The "Deliver the results" stage is focused on implementing the solutions developed during the innovation process. This stage is where the ideas and strategies are put into action to achieve tangible outcomes.

241. Answer: a. Generate the mindset.

Explanation: "Generate the mindset" involves transforming challenges into opportunities by using tools like an IQ assessment. This essential is about creating a strategic mindset that can navigate complex issues and find innovative solutions.

242. Answer: b. To acquire the right information about the environment.

Explanation: Based on the information available about Knowledge Wizard® software, its primary purpose is to assist in gathering and processing information to understand a specific situation or problem. This aligns with the concept of acquiring the right information about the environment.

243. Answer: c. Designing comprehensive solutions.

Explanation: The "Create the solutions" stage involves designing comprehensive solutions that address the problems or opportunities identified in earlier stages. This stage is crucial for developing actionable plans that can be implemented effectively.

244. Answer: b. Communicator.

Explanation: The "Communicator" personality is associated with building loyalty and trust. This role focuses on effective communication, relationship-building, and fostering a collaborative environment.

245. Answer: b. Radical transformation of mind and practices.

Explanation: A successful Kaikaku results in a radical transformation of mindsets and practices, leading to significant improvements in an

Answers

organization's operations. It goes beyond incremental changes and aims for a profound shift in approach.

246. Answer: c. Generating ideas and strategies

Explanation: The "Innovator" in the 20-20 innovation process is responsible for generating new ideas and developing strategies that drive innovation. This role is crucial for ensuring that the process remains forward-thinking and creative.

247. Answer: c. Customer demand and flow of materials.

Explanation: When designing a Lean facility layout, it's important to consider customer demand and the flow of materials. This ensures that the layout supports efficient operations and meets the needs of the customers effectively.

248. Answer: b. It drives the organization's processes and layout.

Explanation: In Lean principles, customer demand is a primary driver of the organization's processes and layout. The goal is to align operations with what customers need, ensuring that processes are efficient and value-driven.

249. Answer: a. Point of Use Storage.

Explanation: "POUS" stands for point-of-use storage, which refers to storing materials and tools close to where they are needed in the production process. Minimizing unnecessary movement and handling reduces waste, improves efficiency, and supports Lean principles.

250. Answer: b. Inventory control.

Explanation: Inventory control is a major consideration in creating a mixed-model pull system. The system needs to be designed to manage varying demands while minimizing inventory levels, which is a key aspect of Lean manufacturing.

Answers

251. Answer: b. Asking about alternatives and eliminations
Explanation:

Playmakers focus on exploring alternatives and considering what can be eliminated to drive change effectively. They challenge the status quo and seek opportunities for innovation and improvement within the organization.

252. Answer: c. Choose destinations and set directions
Explanation:

The first component of managing journeys involves selecting the desired outcomes (destinations) and establishing a clear direction for the organization. This step ensures that all efforts are aligned with the strategic goals.

253. Answer: b. DMADV

Explanation: The PDCA (Plan-Do-Check-Act) cycle is a problem-solving methodology that guides teams through the process of planning, implementing, checking, and acting on solutions. It is used to identify and address issues systematically.

254. Answer: d. Designing solutions that evolve

Explanation: The key to transitioning from a project team to an organizational capability is designing solutions that can evolve. This approach ensures that the solutions remain relevant and adaptable as business needs change.

255. Answer: b. Deliver the results

Explanation: The "Deliver the results" phase focuses on transforming initial success or power into a sustainable competitive advantage. This phase emphasizes consistent execution and scaling solutions to maintain long-term benefits.

256. Answer: c. Intuitive, disciplined execution

Answers

Explanation: The Knowledge Wizard in the delivery results phase emphasizes the importance of executing strategies intuitively but with discipline. This balance ensures that actions are effective and aligned with strategic goals.

257. Answer: a. Simplify and specify

Explanation: The sixth phase of delivering results focuses on actions like setting the pace, piloting the course, and maintaining optimal solutions. "Simplify and specify" is not mentioned as a component of this phase.

258. Answer: b. Fear of the unknown

Explanation: Fear of the unknown is a significant obstacle in Lean Six Sigma (LSS) process improvements. It can cause resistance to change, hindering the successful implementation of LSS methodologies.

259. Answer: b. Small process improvement projects

Explanation: Kaizen is primarily associated with continuous improvement through small, incremental changes. It focuses on making minor adjustments that collectively lead to significant improvements over time.

260. Answer: b. 2 to 4 days or several weeks

Explanation: Kaizen team activities typically last 2 to 4 days or can extend over several weeks, depending on the scope and complexity of the improvement project. These activities are intense, focused, and aimed at quick wins.

261. Answer: d. Kakushin

Explanation: Kakushin reflects the advanced knowledge of Lean Six Sigma (LSS) practitioners. It involves radical innovation and transformation, going beyond small improvements to create breakthrough changes in processes.

262. Answer: b. The entire value stream

Answers

Explanation: The transformation of mind concept enables practitioners to think and act across the entire value stream. This holistic approach ensures that improvements are made throughout the process, from start to finish.

263. Answer: c. Standardized approach to change

Explanation: A standardized approach to change is crucial for systematic innovation. It provides a consistent framework that ensures changes are implemented effectively across the organization.

264. Answer: b. 10-10 innovation process

Explanation: The 10-10 innovation process is designed to demonstrate the six essentials of innovation. It is a structured approach that helps organizations develop and implement innovative solutions systematically.

265. Answer: b. Control chart

Explanation: A control chart helps differentiate between special cause variation (unusual or non-routine events) and common cause variation (inherent in the process). This insight is crucial for determining the right improvement actions.

266. Answer: c. Execute the strategy

Explanation: "Execute the strategy" is not listed as an essential innovation in the 20-20 process. Instead, the process emphasizes creating solutions, delivering results, and managing the journeys.

267. Answer: b. Designing, building, and maintaining optimal solutions

Explanation: The "Create the solutions" stage involves designing, building, and maintaining optimal solutions for the organization. This stage is critical for ensuring that the solutions developed are effective and sustainable.

268. Answer: a. Define, Measure, Analyze, Design, Verify

Answers

Explanation: DMADV stands for Define, Measure, Analyze, Design, Verify. It is a methodology used in Lean Six Sigma to design new processes or products that meet specific customer needs and quality requirements.

269. **Answer: a. fail small and early**

Explanation: Organizations should learn to fail small and early to win big later on. This approach minimizes risk by allowing for early detection of issues, enabling quick adjustments before larger investments are made.

270. **Answer: c. Waste**

Explanation: Employees are expected to systematically eliminate waste by deploying change management concepts. This focus on waste reduction is central to improving efficiency and achieving better results in Lean Six Sigma.

271. **Answer: a. Do we have the right people and capability skill sets behind it?**

Explanation: A key question during the solution creation phase is whether the right people with the necessary skills and capabilities are involved. Having the right team is essential for successfully developing and implementing solutions.

272. **Answer: c. Right information**

Explanation: During the solution creation phase, it is crucial to provide the right information to the right people. Accurate and timely information enables team members to make informed decisions and contribute effectively to the project.

273. **Answer: b. Sustainable advantage through implementation**

Explanation: The "Deliver the results" stage concentrates on achieving a sustainable advantage through the effective implementation of solutions. This phase ensures that the organization benefits from long-term success and improved performance.

Answers

274. Answer: c. Simplifying processes

Explanation: Simplifying processes is a key element of disciplined execution in the delivery results phase. By streamlining workflows and removing unnecessary complexity, organizations can execute strategies more efficiently and effectively.

275. Answer: c. Design, build, and maintain optimal solutions using DMADV

Explanation: A key component of the fifth phase of creating solutions is designing, building, and maintaining optimal solutions using the DMADV methodology. This approach ensures that the solutions are well-structured and aligned with quality standards.

276. Answer: b. To ensure timely and effective execution

Explanation: Setting the pace and piloting the course in the delivery results phase ensures timely and effective execution. This step helps maintain momentum and keep the project on track.

277. Answer: c. Larger scope process improvement projects

Explanation: Kaizen teams' main objective is to tackle larger-scope process improvement projects through continuous, incremental changes. These teams work collaboratively to identify and implement improvements that lead to significant benefits over time.

278. Answer: b. Solving the right problems at the right time

Explanation: The "Manage the Journeys" phase involves identifying and addressing the most critical problems at the appropriate time. This ensures that resources are focused on the issues that will have the greatest impact on the organization's success.

279. Answer: b. Unexpected events

Answers

Explanation: In the journey management phase, organizations should plan for unexpected events. This proactive approach helps minimize disruptions and maintain momentum toward achieving strategic goals.

280. **Answer: b. Conduct a root cause analysis to identify the factors affecting process capability**

Explanation: Before making improvements, it is crucial to understand the root causes of the low process capability. This analysis will help in identifying specific issues that need to be addressed to enhance the process performance effectively.

281. **Answer: b. Bill Smith**

Explanation: Bill Smith of Motorola originated the term Six Sigma when he convinced William J. Weisz that the standard of performance for all business activities should be 3.4 defects per million opportunities.

282. **Answer: d. 3.4 defects per million opportunities**

Explanation: Motorola defines the Six Sigma performance standard as 3.4 defects per million opportunities. This rigorous standard aims to achieve near-perfection in process performance.

283. **Answer: b. Cpk = 1.5**

Explanation: Motorola set a long-term process capability target of Cpk = 1.5. This target reflects the desired level of process capability to ensure consistent quality and minimal defects over time.

284. **Answer: c. Plus or minus Six Sigma**

Explanation: Statistically, 'Six Sigma' refers to a process that operates within six standard deviations (sigma) from the mean. This level of control is associated with extremely low defect rates, aiming for near-perfect quality.

Answers

285. Answer: c. Shewhart

Explanation: Walter A. Shewhart is known for setting the standard of performance in control charts as plus or minus three sigma. His work laid the foundation for modern Statistical Process Control (SPC).

286. Answer: a. PDCA cycle

Explanation: Motorola implemented Six Sigma concepts using the PDCA (Plan-Do-Check-Act) cycle. This iterative process is essential for continuous improvement and effective problem-solving in quality management.

287. Answer: c. RDMAICSI

Explanation: Dr. Mikel Harry from Motorola modified Shewhart's PDCA cycle and developed the RDMAICSI methodology, which stands for Recognize, Define, Measure, Analyze, Improve, Control, Standardize, and Integrate.

288. Answer: b. Six Sigma

Explanation: Six Sigma focuses on reducing variation around the midpoint of a specification. By controlling variability, the goal is to achieve process consistency and reduce defects.

289. Answer: a. Six Sigma Black Belt

Explanation: SSBB stands for Six Sigma Black Belt. This certification level indicates advanced expertise in Six Sigma methodologies and the ability to lead complex projects aimed at process improvement.

290. Answer: c. US$1 million

Explanation: A Six Sigma Black Belt (SSBB) is expected to generate a minimum annual savings of US$500,000 through their direct activities. This financial impact underscores the value of Six Sigma projects to the organization.

Answers

291. Answer: a. 35%

Explanation: An SSBB typically spends about 35% of their time teaching either formally or informally. This teaching role is crucial for spreading Six Sigma knowledge and skills throughout the organization.

292. Answer: d. Software development

Explanation: The skills required for an SSBB include project management, leadership, analytical thinking, adult learning, organizational change management, and statistical analysis, but not software development.

293. Answer: b. 2 years

Explanation: The typical assignment for a Six Sigma Black Belt (SSBB) lasts about 2 years. During this period, the SSBB is expected to lead projects, mentor others, and contribute significantly to process improvement efforts.

294. Answer: a. 1 SSBB

Explanation: The recommended ratio is 1 Six Sigma Black Belt (SSBB) for every 100 employees. This ensures that there are enough skilled individuals to lead and support Six Sigma initiatives across the organization.

295. Answer: c. Six Sigma Yellow Belt

Explanation: The Six Sigma Yellow Belt is considered the first level of training in the Six Sigma hierarchy. Yellow Belts have a basic understanding of Six Sigma concepts and typically support improvement projects within their teams.

296. Answer: a. Define, Measure, Analyze, Improve, Control

Explanation: DMAIC stands for Define, Measure, Analyze, Improve, Control. It is a data-driven methodology used in Six Sigma for improving existing processes by identifying and eliminating defects.

Answers

297. Answer: b. Prioritize root cause based on their impact and feasibility

Explanation: Prioritizing root causes allows the team to focus on the most critical issues that will yield the greatest improvement. Addressing all root causes simultaneously may lead to resource overload and diminished effectiveness.

298. Answer: d. Toyota

Explanation: Toyota is credited with refining Lean concepts and developing the Toyota Production System (TPS), which is widely regarded as one of the most effective auto assembly processes in the world. Their focus on eliminating waste, continuous improvement, and customer value has revolutionized manufacturing practices globally.

299. Answer: b. Analyze the necessity of each non-value-added step

Explanation: Before eliminating steps, it's essential to analyze their necessity and understand their context in the process. This ensures that no critical steps are removed inadvertently and that improvements are sustainable.

300. Answer: b. To design new processes

Explanation: DMADV (Define, Measure, Analyze, Design, Verify) is a Six Sigma methodology specifically focused on designing new products, processes, or services.

It is a structured approach to creating something new that meets customer needs and delivers high quality.

301. Answer: b. Improved customer satisfaction

Explanation: Benchmarking allows organizations to identify best practices and implement them, leading to enhanced performance and improved

Answers

customer satisfaction, which is critical for maintaining competitive advantage.

302. Answer: c. Mixed

Explanation: Benchmarking types include internal, external, and comprehensive. "Mixed" is not a recognized category; comprehensive benchmarking may involve a blend of internal and external approaches.

303. Answer: d. 1980s

Explanation: IBM recognized in the 1980s that adopting the best practices globally could significantly enhance their operations, leading to competitive advantages and efficiency improvements.

304. Answer: b. Fuji-Xerox was selling copiers at manufacturing cost.

Explanation: Xerox found that Fuji-Xerox could sell copiers at the same price as Xerox's manufacturing cost, highlighting the efficiency and cost-management issues within Xerox, which led to significant strategic changes.

305. Answer: b. Xerox

Explanation: Xerox was a pioneer in benchmarking and used it to drive significant improvements, which contributed to winning the prestigious Malcolm Baldrige Award for quality in 1988.

306. Answer: c. Identify what to benchmark

Explanation: The first step in internal benchmarking is to determine which processes or practices to benchmark, setting the foundation for subsequent measurement and comparison.

307. Answer: a. Conduct telephone interviews and surveys

Answers

Explanation: After data exchange, conducting interviews and surveys helps gather more detailed insights and validates the data, ensuring that the benchmarking analysis is thorough and accurate.

308. Answer: b. Reverse engineering

Explanation: Reverse engineering involves deconstructing a competitor's product or process to understand how it works. This provides insights that can be used to improve one's processes.

309. Answer: b. For goal setting and process development

Explanation: Process benchmarking helps organizations understand best practices and set goals for process improvement, leading to more efficient and effective operations.

310. Answer: b. Literature searches

Explanation: Literature searches involve reviewing existing publications, reports, and studies to gather information on external organizations' practices, making it a widely used method for benchmarking.

311. Answer: d. Phase V

Explanation: Phase V focuses on implementing improvements based on benchmarking insights, ensuring that the process or item being benchmarked performs better after incorporating best practices.

312. Answer: a. Ratio measurements

Explanation: Ratio measurements compare different metrics (like efficiency, cost, or time) before and after changes, allowing organizations to assess the impact of benchmarking-driven improvements objectively.

313. Answer: b. Functional benchmarking

Answers

Explanation: Functional benchmarking compares specific processes or functions against those of world-class organizations, even in different industries, to identify and adopt best practices.

314. Answer: c. Benchmark database

Explanation: After collecting and analyzing internal data, the benchmark database should be established and updated.

315. Answer: b. IBM

Explanation: In the 1960s, IBM leveraged best practices from around the world to gain a significant competitive advantage internationally, setting a precedent for modern benchmarking practices.

316. Answer: c. Hold a team meeting to consolidate observations

Explanation: Following a site visit, it's essential to have a team meeting to consolidate observations, ensuring that all insights are captured and discussed for effective benchmarking.

317. Answer: b. Strong leadership

Explanation: Strong leadership is critical for driving the implementation of best practices and fostering a culture of continuous improvement, which is vital for maintaining world-class standards.

318. Answer: c. Develop the data collection plan

Explanation: In Phase II, developing a data collection plan is crucial as it outlines how, when, and where data will be gathered, ensuring that the benchmarking process is systematic and effective.

319. Answer: c. Functional benchmarking

Answers

Explanation: Functional benchmarking involves comparing specific functions or processes with those in dissimilar industries, allowing organizations to adopt innovative practices from diverse fields.

320. **Answer: b. Measurement system**

Explanation: A measurement system should be established to measure the impact of changes in the benchmarking process.

321. **Answer: c. Discovering methods for process improvement**

Explanation: Process benchmarking aims to identify and implement methods for improving processes, making operations more efficient, and enhancing overall performance.

322. **Answer: c. To prioritize implementation activities**

Explanation: The primary goal of a change-impact analysis is to assess which changes will have the most significant positive effect and prioritize them for implementation.

323. **Answer: a. Encyclopedia of Trade Associations**

Explanation: The Encyclopedia of Trade Associations is a valuable resource for identifying relevant trade and professional associations and aiding in the selection of benchmarking partners.

324. **Answer: b. Type of industry**

Explanation: The type of industry is a key factor in external benchmarking as it ensures that comparisons are made with organizations facing similar challenges and market conditions.

325. **Answer: b. Cost per unit**

Answers

Explanation: Cost per unit is an effort-related measurement as it reflecting the resources expended to produce a single unit. It provides insights into process efficiency and effectiveness.

326. **Answer: b. Increase monitoring and measurement of key metrics**

Explanation: Strengthening the monitoring and measurement of key metrics helps ensure that the process stays on track and improvements are sustained. It allows for timely identification of issues before they escalate.

327. **Answer: b. Understand the product, process, or activity to be benchmarked**

Explanation: Before data generation, it is critical to have a thorough understanding of the process or activity being benchmarked, ensuring that the data collected is relevant and meaningful.

328. **Answer: c. Quantitative data**

Explanation: Quantitative data, which includes measurable metrics like time, cost, and efficiency, is essential for managing and controlling processes in benchmarking, providing a solid basis for comparison.

329. **Answer: c. They allow data exchange without disclosing sensitive information.**

Explanation: Ratio measurements provide a way to compare performance without revealing confidential details, making them useful in benchmarking where sensitive data might be involved.

330. **Answer: c. Obtaining management support**

Explanation: After identifying what to benchmark, securing management support is crucial, as it ensures that the necessary resources and backing are available for the benchmarking process.

Answers

331. Answer: b. Enhance efficiency and effectiveness

Explanation: The primary goal of bureaucracy elimination is to enhance efficiency and effectiveness by removing unnecessary steps and delays in business processes.

332. Answer: b. Symmetry and beauty of design

Explanation: Streamlining suggests an ultimate search for efficiency and effectiveness, implying symmetry, harmony of elements, and beauty of design.

333. Answer: b. Process-focused approach

Explanation: The process-focused approach involves flowcharting a process to identify and eliminate bureaucratic steps.

334. Answer: b. Paranoia about being blamed for errors

Explanation: Paranoia about being blamed for errors is one of the psychological factors contributing to bureaucracy.

335. Answer: c. 90%

Explanation: Studies have shown that up to 90% of documents retained by organizations are never used again. This highlights the inefficiency of excessive documentation and the importance of reducing unnecessary paperwork as part of bureaucracy elimination efforts.

336. Answer: c. IBM, San Jose, California

Explanation: IBM, in San Jose, California, established a bureaucracy elimination committee to scrutinize and eliminate unnecessary activities within the organization. This initiative was part of a broader effort to improve efficiency by eliminating the redundant processes.

337. Answer: a. Blue highlighter

Answers

Explanation: In the process-focused approach, a blue highlighter is often used to mark bureaucratic steps in a flowchart. This visual tool helps quickly identify steps that add little to no value, making it easier to eliminate them.

338. Answer: b. 2:1

Explanation: A 2:1 return on investment is typically required to justify retaining a bureaucratic activity. This means the benefits of the activity should at least double the costs involved in maintaining it to be considered worthwhile.

339. Answer: c. It gets the total organization involved

Explanation: The incident-focused approach to bureaucracy elimination is advantageous because it involves the entire organization, not just management. This inclusive approach ensures that employees at all levels contribute to identifying and eliminating unnecessary bureaucratic practices.

340. Answer: c. The reasons for its existence and impact on the organization

Explanation: Before eliminating a bureaucratic operation, it is crucial to understand the reasons for its existence and its impact on the organization. This ensures that essential functions are not removed without considering their importance or potential consequences.

341. Answer: c. Saved $60 million a year

Explanation: Intel's initiative to eliminate unnecessary bureaucracy resulted in significant cost savings, amounting to $60 million per year. This demonstrates the financial benefits of streamlining processes and reducing inefficiencies.

342. Answer: b. Bad, boring, burdensome, brutal

Answers

Explanation: In the context of bureaucracy, "Big B" refers to the negative aspects of bureaucratic processes—bad, boring, burdensome, and brutal. These characteristics are often used to describe the cumbersome nature of excessive bureaucracy.

343. Answer: c. 40-50%

Explanation: Managers typically spend 40-50% of their time dealing with job-related materials, such as paperwork and administrative tasks. Eliminating unnecessary bureaucratic processes can reduce this significant time investment.

344. Answer: c. Adds resistance to progress

Explanation: Bureaucracy often impedes progress by introducing unnecessary layers of approval and administrative steps, which slow down decision-making and impede organizational efficiency.

345. Answer: b. Data and cost-benefit analysis

Explanation: Justifying the retention of a bureaucratic step should be based on data and a cost-benefit analysis. This approach ensures that only steps that provide clear value and justify their costs are maintained.

346. Answer: c. Minimizing unnecessary steps

Explanation: When identifying bureaucracy in a process, the focus should be on minimizing unnecessary steps that do not add value. Eliminating these steps can streamline the process and lead to greater efficiency and effectiveness.

347. Answer: b. Elimination of 50 unnecessary procedures

Explanation: IBM, Brazil, demonstrated a significant outcome of bureaucracy elimination by removing 50 unnecessary procedures. This action helped streamline operations, improve efficiency, and reduce administrative burdens.

Answers

348. Answer: d. Bureaucracy elimination

Explanation: Bureaucracy elimination is not typically used as a conflict resolution technique. Conflict resolution usually involves techniques like arbitration, mediation, and litigation to resolve disputes between parties.

349. Answer: c. Be proactive

Explanation: Stephen Covey's model for conflict resolution begins with the habit of "Being proactive." This habit emphasizes taking initiative and responsibility for one's actions, which is crucial in resolving conflicts effectively.

350. Answer: b. Analyzing characteristics important to the customer

Explanation: Critical to Quality (CTQ) analysis is used to identify and analyze characteristics that are important to the customer. This ensures that the final product or service meets customer expectations and quality standards.

About Our Products

Other products from VERSAtile Reads are:

 Elevate Your Leadership: The 10 Must-Have Skills

 Elevate Your Leadership: 8 Effective Communication Skills

 Elevate Your Leadership: 10 Leadership Styles for Every Situation

 300+ PMP Practice Questions Aligned with PMBOK 7, Agile Methods, and Key Process Groups – 2024

 Exam-Cram Essentials Last-Minute Guide to Ace the PMP Exam - Your Express Guide featuring PMBOK® Guide

 Career Mastery Blueprint - Strategies for Success in Work and Business

 Memory Magic: Unraveling the Secret of Mind Mastery

 The Success Equation Psychological Foundations For Accomplishment

 Fairy Dust Chronicles – The Short and Sweet of Wonder

 B2B Breakthrough – Proven Strategies from Real-World Case Studies

Copyright © 2024 VERSAtile Reads. All rights reserved.
This material is protected by copyright, any infringement will be dealt with legal and punitive action.

About Our Products

 CISSP Fast Track Master: CISSP Essentials for Exam Success

 CISA Fast Track Master: CISA Essentials for Exam Success

 CISM Fast Track Master: CISM Essentials for Exam Success

 CCSP Fast Track Master: CCSP Essentials for Exam Success

 CLF-C02: AWS Certified Cloud Practitioner: Fast Track to Exam Success

 ITIL 4 Foundation Essentials: Fast Track to Exam Success

 CCNP Security Essentials: Fast Track to Exam Success

 Certified SCRUM Master Exam Cram Essentials

Copyright © 2024 VERSAtile Reads. All rights reserved.
This material is protected by copyright, any infringement will be dealt with legal and punitive action.

About Our Products

Copyright © 2024 VERSAtile Reads. All rights reserved.
This material is protected by copyright, any infringement will be dealt with legal and punitive action.

www.ingramcontent.com/pod-product-compliance
Lightning Source LLC
Chambersburg PA
CBHW080456220526
45465CB00006B/2289